W9-CIR-954

Choosing a Healthcare Career

Becoming a Healthcare Professional

Jane John-Nwankwo CPT, RN, MSN, PHN

Choosing a Healthcare Career: Becoming a Healthcare Professional

ISBN-13: 978-1484151013

ISBN-10: 1484151011

Printed in the United States of America.

Dedication

Dedicated to my mother, Patricia Onwere who gave me all the love I needed in my childhood and encouraged me to be a nurse.

OTHER TITLES FROM THE SAME AUTHOR:

1. Director of Staff Development: The Nurse Educator

2. Crisis Prevention & Intervention in Healthcare: Management of Assaultive Behavior

3. CNA Exam Prep: Nurse Assistant Practice Test Questions. Vol. One & Two

4. Patient Care Technician Exam Certification Review Questions: PCT Test Prep

5. IV Therapy & Blood Withdrawal Review Questions

6. Medical Assistant Test Preparation

7. EKG Test Prep

8. Phlebotomy Test Prep

9. The Home Health Aide Textbook

10. How to make a million in nursing

11. Home Health Aide Exam Prep

Order these books now at www.bestamericanhealthed.com/resources.html
Or call 951 637 8332 for bulk purchases

SELF ASSESSMENT QUESTIONNAIRE FOR HEALTHCARE PROFESSIONS

1. Do I like working with children?

2. Do I enjoy working with the elderly?

3. Can I handle the mentally disabled?

4. Am I afraid of needles?

5. Can I change soiled adult diapers comfortably?

6. How do I feel when handling someone else's body products?

7. How do I feel when someone tells me they are in pain?

8. Do sick people irritate me?

9. Do I prefer to do paper work while other people do the care?

10. Am I happy working with numbers and billing figures?

11. Do I enjoy auditing paper work?

12. Do I prefer caring for people in their own homes?

13. Do I prefer caring for people in a group setting?

14. Do I want to just deal with the computation of the medication and leave the administration to someone else?

15. How do I feel in the sight of blood?

16. How do I feel with the sight of an open wound?

17. Can I really work under stress and be organized knowing that someone's life may just depend on my decision?

18. Am I very careful and feel that I can observe the precautions not to transmit infection to myself and my family?

The good news is that the healthcare profession is very versatile and can accommodate a variety of skills.

TABLE OF CONTENTS

Introduction

As the owner of two healthcare educational institutions, I often come in contact with anxiety-filled faces of individuals who really would like to become healthcare professionals but do not know which career to choose. I have seen many cases of individuals switching from one course to another and later settling for the third course where they think they have found their nitch. In one case, I had a student who wanted to draw blood but fainted during the introductory video on phlebotomy. She fainted because she saw blood in the TV! I advised her to change her course. This book has been written as an informational material for individuals choosing to start with the entry level healthcare courses. I purposely left out the more advanced courses. More than 10 entry-level healthcare courses have been explained in this book to aid the prospective healthcare professional in making an informed choice while considering their personal strengths and weaknesses. It is best to have a career that gives one fulfillment, not just a job to pay one's bills. For speaking appointments for your organization on this topic and other healthcare topics, please email jane@dignityeducationalconsulting.com

Jane John-Nwankwo CPT, RN, RM, MSN, PHN

Advantages and disadvantages of being a healthcare professional

1. **Introduction.**

Choosing a career can be an overwhelming task, and will require careful consideration of different choices. Healthcare is one field that can offer successful careers and has been persistent over the years. Below are ten advantages and ten disadvantages of the healthcare profession.

2. **Advantages of being a healthcare professional.**

The healthcare profession is considered a noble career since it gives care to people in need selflessly. Healthcare professionals take care of the ill patients and understand how their physical health connects with their emotions. The healthcare professional bears in mind the interest of the patient as they continue a loving culture that is passed on from generation to generation.

Lesmeister (2006, p. 11) mentions that the healthcare profession deals with situations concerning the health of individuals. Every day new patients come in with diverse needs. Being able to offer assistance gives a positive experience each time .

Healthcare professionals are involved in making decisions about life. Besides participating in treating patients to restore health and save lives of the sick and the injured, they are concerned promoting healthy living to prevent illnesses. The contribution to healthy living impacts communities when they are able to treat diseases and healthcare conditions.

The healthcare profession provides an opportunity for growth. Healthcare professionals have a variety of opportunities where they can offer their services. Experienced healthcare professionals often see the opportunity to train others.

The healthcare industry provides the healthcare professionals with stability and security that people look for in a career. There is a growing need for healthcare professionals to assist with the increasing healthcare needs of the society. The population is constantly increasing with many people seeking healthcare. The care needed ranges from new born babies to the aging parents. Therefore, the chance of a healthcare professional staying without a job is very minimal.

Opportunities emerging in the healthcare profession absorb the graduates from different fields in healthcare. After varied periods of study, students who successfully complete their programs are absorbed in the healthcare industry within a short period of time. This is because all levels of education ranging from certificate to post graduate programs pass through what is popularly known as 'hands-on training'. This method of training provides not only theory, but practical training, ensuring that graduates are more prepared for the job.

There are a variety of options for healthcare professionals. Individuals who like figures can go into billing and coding. Baby lovers can work in pediatrics. Those who like caring for people in their homes can choose home health. Do you have a passion to care for the mentally disabled? Mental health maybe your best choice. Like being part of people coming into the world? Maternal and child health could work out for you. The aspect of having a variety of choices aids healthcare professionals in obtaining personal fulfillment. The professional's experiences include changing the lives of people on a daily basis.

The demand for healthcare professionals is very high because of the emerging ailments in the increasing population. Since healthcare professionals are on demand their compensation is also high. Healthcare professionals with more skills are paid higher than those with minimal skills.

The healthcare profession allows healthcare workers to travel. Patients are found in different locations; hence, healthcare professionals are distributed in different locations in the world. The arrangements to travel can be made if the healthcare professional is willing to travel (Gerdin, 2011, p. 7). An example of this is the travel nurse positions where a hospital in a different location hires a nurse for a 13-week contract, pays them a little higher than the regular staff and gives them the option to renew the contract when it is over.

3. **Disadvantages of being a healthcare professional Conclusion.**

While working as a healthcare professional can be fulfilling, the nature of work can be physically demanding. Healthcare professionals carry along medical equipment and resources (**Learning Express Editors** 2010, p. 8).

Depending on the tasks to be performed, healthcare professionals may end up standing up and walking for hours. Makely et al (2013, p. 5) notes that, working for long hours causes strain on the back and neck. The nature of work might involve moving or lifting patients to transfer them to the correct location or position. Healthcare professionals sometimes ask for assistance from other professionals to transfer patients when the task is burdensome in given situations. When the patient needs immediate attention or the medical equipment is not appropriate for the given situation, healthcare professionals transfer the patient physically.

Even though resources are invested into education about proper body techniques, healthcare professionals still become victims of injury on the job resulting from patient transfer. I recall few years ago, working as a nurse in an intensive care unit, I had an over-weight patient. Even though I asked for assistance to move her during my care, I still broke my wrist. I suffered from the wrist pain for more than one year.

Becoming a healthcare professional may require one to spend some of their holidays saving patients' lives. This includes working on holidays in hospital units, treating patients and attending to emergencies. Although some departments may have arrangements to close on holidays, other departments must remain open. The healthcare professionals working in the hospitals would definitely have to sacrifice some holidays.

Healthcare professionals work in various shifts. Some healthcare facilities are open twenty four hours a day, seven days of the week. The shifts are dependent on the setting of the healthcare facility. Shift hours may not be favorable. Night shift requires the nurse to keep awake all night; this may not be an easy task.

Sometimes, one may be required to work overtime if their partner fails to show up for their shift.

Emergencies may call for extended hours if there is shortage of workers when the work load increases. Holidays, weekends and days-off may be cut short by emergencies if there is shortage of healthcare workers. There is usually a decreased amount of time spent with family and friends. Many over-dedicated healthcare workers end up losing their marriages because while they were busy saving other peoples' lives, they deprived their loved ones the required love and attention they needed.

Handling shifts and emergencies may not be comfortable to some people. Adjusting to the strenuous shifts can be a daunting task. While working on a night-shift means that the healthcare should be awake and alert to perform their duties, day- shift requires the worker to leave very early to report to work. For an individual that has small children, she may not see her kids during the day at all on some days.

Healthcare professionals are the first victim of angered patients. Patients with assaultive behavior may hurt the healthcare professionals (Swanson, 2005, p. 67). This is especially true for units like emergency rooms, mental health units, etc.

4. Conclusion

The benefit of being in healthcare profession is ability to connect physical and emotional needs, change lives and impact communities. There is stability, opportunity for growth, availability of work, training opportunity, and progress in career, room for specialization, personal fulfillment, traveling opportunities and competent compensation. However, healthcare profession can be physically demanding, tiring, require long working hours and exposure to assaultive patients.

Section Two

This section tries to give a brief explanation about different entry-level healthcare professions.

NURSE ASSISTANT (CNA)

This is usually an entry level for individuals who wish to become nurses in the future. Students are taught principles of infection control, communication techniques, and the skills to safely care for people. These skills include bathing, dressing, assisting to eat, grooming, toileting, lifting and moving while using proper body mechanics.

Upon completion of this course, students will be able to:

Technical Skills

- Demonstrate awareness of industry standards.
- Define Title 22 regulations regarding the rights of patients.
- Follow hospital safety rules; discuss the role of a nurse assistant in an emergency.
- Practice proper use of body mechanics and positioning techniques using devises for patient comfort and safety.
- Practice centigrade and Fahrenheit conversions for weight, length and liquid volume.
- Demonstrate ability to bathe, dress, and perform personal hygiene tasks for patients.
- Demonstrate ability to collect specimens, remove urinary catheters, apply dressings and make beds.
- Take temperature, pulse and respiration; take accurate blood pressure; document findings.
- Distinguish between types of diet therapies; serve and feed patients.
- Recognize signs and symptoms of distress; react and intervene appropriately.
- Demonstrate ability to care for patients with neurological disorders and aged residents.
- Assist patient with rehabilitative processes and with activities of daily living.

Personal and Professional Skills

- Discuss disinfection and sterilization, hazardous waste disposal, and standard precautions.

- Demonstrate effective patient care documentation.

- Discuss stages of dying and related care; interaction with families; and post-mortem care.

- Demonstrate appropriate work ethics and professional demeanor as demanded by the industry.

- Demonstrate the ability to work independently or as a member of a team.

- Listen attentively, follow directions and effectively relay directions to others.

Career Planning Skills

- Research career opportunities; establish educational and career goals related to the health care industry.

- Research employment opportunities; prepare a resume; prepare for an interview.

When preparing to sit for the state exam as a CNA, I would highly recommend my books: CNA Exam Prep Volume One and Two

HOME HEALTH AIDE

Duties

A Home Health Aide is an essential member of a healthcare team. Under the supervision of a licensed nurse, they may bathe, dress, feed, mobilize and transport people; obtain temperature, pulse and blood pressure measurements; and report observations and reactions. Other duties may include preparation of equipment, care of the patient's room and record keeping. The home Health Aide functions as a home maker for the clients helping the client leave in the comfort of their own homes while they are rehabilitating.

At the conclusion of the Home Health Aide program, the student sits for a completion exam at the training school. If successful, student will receive their state certificate within few weeks from the State registry. While undergoing your training as a Home Health Aide, I highly recommend two of my books: The Home Health Aide Textbook and Home Health Aide Exam Prep.

There are two types of home health aide programs:

1. Minimum of 40 hours for individuals who are already Certified Nurse Assistants

2. Minimum of $75 hours for individuals who are not Certified Nurse Assistants (depends on state requirements)

Program Description

The Home Health Aide program consists of theory hours and hours of clinical experience in a skilled nursing facility or a home health care setting.

Program Admission Requirements

- Program application
- Health Form and Immunization documentation
- 16 years of age
- Caregiver background check
- Mandatory orientation
- Financial competence

-

Program Outcomes

- Placement on the state Registry (if student successfully passes the final test)

- Provides safe care to a diverse client population and meets physical and psychosocial client needs.

- Effectively uses verbal, nonverbal and written communication skills to communicate with all clients and families, document client information and communicate with members of the home health agency team.

- Works cooperatively in a team environment.

- Demonstrates ethical/legal behavior by functioning under the direct supervision of a designated health care professional.

- Displays professional behavior and is accountable for his/her own actions.

Caregiver Background Check: Must meet guidelines established by the state statutes regarding aide and technician background check information in order to be eligible for state certification.

More Information

The student will find the Home health Aide program to be a very rewarding experience. In addition to attending to the personal needs of adult and geriatric clients, he/she will also learn how to carry out their personal plans of care as they relate to their safety, comfort, nutrition and elimination needs, psychosocial well-being, basic restorative care, adaptations for the home environment and hospice care. Focus will be on the special needs of the elderly at home.

EKG TECHNICIAN

DESCRIPTION: The Electrocardiograph Technician program provides an overview of basic cardiovascular terminology, anatomy and physiology. Focuses on the proper placement of electrocardiogram (EKG) leads and maintenance of equipment to obtain an accurate 12-Lead EKG. Learn to recognize cardiac arrhythmias. The course teaches responsibilities of ECG\EKG technicians and provides clinical laboratory opportunity to develop entry level skills.

COURSE PREREQUISITE(S): none

NATURE OF THE EKG TECHNICIAN WORK

Cardiovascular technicians who obtain EKGs are known as *electrocardiograph* (or *EKG) technicians.* To take a basic EKG, which traces electrical impulses transmitted by the heart, technicians attach electrodes to the patient's chest, arms, and legs, and then manipulate switches on an EKG machine to obtain a reading. A printout is made for interpretation by the physician. This test is done before most kinds of surgery or as part of a routine physical examination, especially for persons who have reached middle age or who have a history of cardiovascular problems.

EKG technicians with advanced training perform Holter monitor and stress testing. For Holter monitoring, technicians place electrodes on the patient's chest and attach a portable EKG monitor to the patient's belt. Following 24 or more hours of normal activity by the patient, the technician removes a tape from the monitor and places it in a scanner. After checking the quality of the recorded impulses on an electronic screen, the technician usually prints the information from the tape so that a physician can interpret it later. Physicians use the output from the scanner to diagnose heart ailments, such as heart rhythm abnormalities or problems with pacemakers.

For a treadmill stress test, EKG technicians document the patient's medical history, explain the procedure, connect the patient to an EKG monitor, and obtain a baseline reading and resting blood pressure. Next, they monitor the heart's performance while the patient is walking on a treadmill, gradually increasing the treadmill's speed to observe the effect of increased exertion. Like vascular technologists and cardiac sonographers, cardiographic technicians who perform EKG, Holter monitor, and stress tests are known as "noninvasive" technicians.

Some EKG technicians schedule appointments, type doctors' interpretations, maintain patient files, and care for equipment

WORKING CONDITIONS

EKG technicians generally work a 5-day, 40-hour week that may include weekends. Those in catheterization labs tend to work longer hours and may work evenings. They also may be on call during the night and on weekends.

EKG technicians spend a lot of time walking and standing. Those who work in catheterization labs may face stressful working conditions because they are in close contact with patients with serious heart ailments. Some patients, for example, may encounter complications from time to time that have life-or-death implications.

EMPLOYMENT

About 3 out 4 jobs are in hospitals, primarily in cardiology departments. The remaining jobs are mostly in offices of physicians, including cardiologists; or in medical and diagnostic laboratories, including diagnostic imaging centers.

TRAINING, OTHER QUALIFICATIONS, AND ADVANCEMENT

For basic EKGs, Holter monitoring, and stress testing, few months certification programs exist, but most EKG technicians are still trained on the job by an EKG supervisor or a cardiologist. On-the-job training usually lasts about 8 to 16 weeks. Most employers prefer to train people already in the healthcare field—nursing aides, for example. EKG Technicians usually undergo a minimum of a 60 hour training. They may be working part time to gain experience and make contact with employers.

EKG technicians must be reliable, have mechanical aptitude, and be able to follow detailed instructions. A pleasant, relaxed manner for putting patients at ease is an asset.

The following topics are covered in the EKG Technician curriculum:

Fundamentals of Medical Assisting

This is an introductory course for the Medical Assistant program. This course places emphasis on patient-centered assessment, examination, intervention and treatment as directed by a physician. It includes vital signs, collection and documentation of patient information, asepsis, minor surgical procedures and other treatments appropriate for the medical office. Medical office procedures and customer service will be discussed. Administrative and clinical competencies are presented. Students will be required to demonstrate proficiency in these skills.

Medical Anatomy and Physiology

This course is a study of human anatomy and physiology. Lectures systematically take the student from the microscopic level through the formation of organ systems, with emphasis on the interdependence of these systems. Functional concepts and internal structure are related to surface anatomy as a basis for performing a physical examination. The physiology lectures will provide the overall physiology of the human body but will also relate how that physiology breaks down or malfunctions in time of infection, disease, trauma, and aging.

Medical Terminology

This course is a study of a medical assistant of a medical vocabulary system. It includes structure, recognition, analysis, definition, spelling, pronunciation, and combination of medical terms from prefixes, suffixes, roots and combining forms.

Medical Law and Ethics

This is a course of instruction in principles, procedures, and regulations involving legal and ethical relationships among physicians, patients, and medical assistants. It includes current ethical issues as they relate to the practice of medicine and conformity responsibilities. This is a writing intensive course.

Asepsis and Infection Control

This course is a study of standard protocol for the protection of the health care worker and patient to ensure that the procedures and treatments prescribed by the physician are performed properly and safely to assist in the patients return to health.

CPR and First Aid

This course will cover the theory and practical skills of the standard first aid course prescribed by the American Red Cross, American Heart association or other recognized bodies. The focus of this course will provide a general understanding of the needs of the injured person and, in doing so, give care to the person including CPR until medical help is obtained.

Introduction to EKG

This course introduces students to patient preparation, EKG machines, performing and mounting of 12 lead, single channel EKG tracings. Review of the cardiovascular system and related terminology. Emphasis on basic rhythm identification and possible disease states.

Applied EKG

Advanced knowledge of the cardiovascular system with emphasis on the heart in disease states including identification of cardiac arrhythmias using EKG wave form, interpretation of advanced arrhythmias, hypertrophies, cardiac ischemia, and myocardial infarction is discussed.

Clinical EKG

This course provides advanced training which is often required to obtain employment in the field; cardiac stress testing, artificial pacemaker evaluation, 24 hour Holter monitoring and advanced cardiac arrhythmia recognition and telemetry monitoring. Students use equipment which includes the pacemaker simulator, Holter monitor recorders, 3-channel EKG recording systems and telemetry monitors.

HIPAA Compliance

This is a short course of study that discusses the patient's right to privacy, the laws and regulations of the Health Insurance Portability and Accountability Act (HIPAA). The governing bodies that set these standards and penalties provided for non-compliance are also discussed.

Externship

Students are placed in a medical facility where there is an opportunity to observe, assist, learn, and perform patient services in an acute care setting. The externship is an essential component of the program where theoretical and practical skills are integrated. Specific objectives, including cognitive, affective, and psychomotor behaviors must be met for students to complete this course.

Career Development

This course is designed to assist the student in resume development, soft skills, interviewing strategies and decision-making skills to assist the student in obtaining employment. Optional externships are encouraged to offer the student the opportunity for real-life experience.

Certification Exam

I would recommend certifying through the national healthcareer association. In order to become nationally certified as an EKG Technician, you will have to achieve a passing score of 70% or better on the certification exam and prove competency performing an electrocardiogram. When preparing for your EKG Certification exam, I would recommend my EKG Test Preparation Books. Check: www.bestamericanhealthed.com/resources.html

If you are training in a school that follows the National Healthcareer Association curriculum for EKG, at the end of the module,

- The student will demonstrate knowledge of the anatomy and physiology of the Cardiovascular System

- The student will demonstrate knowledge of medical terminology related to EKG.

- The student will be able to identify the phases of the cardiac cycle.

- The student will demonstrate basic understanding of EKG interpretations

- The student will demonstrate the ability to recognize normal and abnormal EKG's.

- The student will become familiar with different ECG equipment.

- The student will be able to properly set up ECG equipment.

- The student will learn proper identification techniques of the patient.

- The student will learn how to introduce him or herself in a professional manner.

- The student will be familiar with the Patient's Bill of Rights.

- The student will list the important information that must be included on the ECG report.

- The student will demonstrate basic understanding of cardiac disorders and emergencies.

- The student will have a basic understanding of the pharmacology of drugs commonly used in the treatment of cardiac disorders.

- The student will demonstrate proficiency in Cardiopulmonary Resuscitation.

- The student will demonstrate proficiency in Electrocardiography (ECG's).

- The student will demonstrate understanding of the theory of EKG by scoring a minimum of 70% on the National Certification written exam.

  Best American Healthcare University Offers online EKG Technician Programs. See

  www.bestamericanhealthcareuni.com or

  http://www.bestamericanhealthed.com/Online-ekg.html

Certified Phlebotomy Technician

SIGNIFICANT POINTS:

- A health occupation in which there is extensive contact with patients.
- Job prospects should be very good, particularly in offices of physicians and blood banks.

NATURE OF THE WORK:

The Phlebotomist is a vital member of the clinical laboratory team, whose main function is to obtain patients' blood specimens by venipuncture and micro collection. The field of Phlebotomy has greatly expanded in the past several years and the role of this team member of the health care team has recently been brought into much sharper focus. The increasingly high amount of laboratory blood testing performed each day; the aging population and the national shortage of registered nurses have caused a dramatic emphasis on the need for highly trained Phlebotomists.

WORKING CONDITIONS AND PHYSICAL EFFORT:

- Work is performed in an interior medical/clinical environment.

- Moderate physical activity. May require physical effort including lifting up to 25 pounds and some extended periods of standing or walking.

- Will work with blood or blood-borne pathogens and will require OSHA training.

DESCRIPTION OF THE PROFESSIONAL COMPETENCIES:

Phlebotomists are proficient in:

1. collecting, transporting, handling and processing blood specimens for analysis;

2. recognizing the importance of specimen collection in the overall patient care system;

3. relating the anatomy and physiology of body systems and anatomic terminology to the major areas of the clinical laboratory, and to general pathologic conditions associated with body systems;

4. identifying and selecting equipment, supplies and additives used in blood collection;

5. recognizing factors that affect specimen collection procedures and test results, and taking appropriate actions within predetermined limits, when applicable;

6. recognizing and adhering to infection control and safety policies and procedures;

7. monitoring quality control within predetermined limits;

8. recognizing the various components of the health care delivery system;

9. recognizing the responsibilities of other laboratory and health care personnel and interacting with them with respect for their jobs and patient care;

10. demonstrating professional conduct, stress management, interpersonal and communication skills with patients, peers and other health care personnel and with the public;

11. demonstrating an understanding of requisitioning and the legal implications of their work environment;

12. applying basic principles in learning new techniques and procedures;

13. Recognizing and acting upon individual needs for continuing education as a function of growth and maintenance of professional competence.

A national certification exam is required for most states. Best American Healthcare University offers an online phlebotomy program for students in every state of the US, except the states of California and Louisiana because of their specific state requirements. The student taking an online phlebotomy program would have to locate a facility for his/her hands-on blood draws. Upon graduation and initial employment, the phlebotomist will be able to demonstrate entry level competencies in the above areas of professional practice.

DESCRIPTION: This course provides phlebotomy instruction to the student with a working knowledge of collecting blood while emphasizing on patient safety, quality assurance, universal and standard precautions.

METHODS OF INSTRUCTION: This course utilizes a lecture, clinical laboratory and demonstration methodology.

COURSE CONTACT HOURS: *Minimum* of 80 contact hours (Classroom/lab).

CRITERIA FOR CERTIFICATION: Students must achieve a minimum of 25 successful venipunctures and 10 capillary sticks. Students must achieve a passing grade of 70% on the National Certification exam.

CURRICULUM

Instructional Areas

The curriculum must include instruction/experiences in the following:

1. 40 hours of theory/classroom instruction

2. 40 hours of applied experiences;

3. Performance of a minimum of 25 successful unaided venipuncture collections;

4. Performance of a minimum of 10 successful unaided capillary collections;

5. Instruction in a variety of collection techniques, including vacuum collection devices, syringe and capillary/skin-puncture methods.

6. Successful completion of Certification exam: Certified Phlebotomy Technician, CPT.

The topics covered include the following:

Introduction to Phlebotomy

Introductory course that explains the function of today's Phlebotomy Technicians. This course identifies the Phlebotomists role on the healthcare team. Students will be introduced to various departments within the laboratory setting and the role of each department.

LEARNING OBJECTIVES

1) Demonstrate knowledge of the health care delivery system and medical terminology.

   a) Identify the health care providers in hospitals and clinics and the phlebotomist's role as a member of this health care team.

   b) Describe the various hospital departments and their major functions in which the phlebotomist may interact in his/her role.

   c) Describe the organizational structure of the clinical laboratory department.

   d) Discuss the roles of the clinical laboratory personnel and their qualifications for these professional positions.

   e) List the types of laboratory procedures performed in the various sections of the clinical laboratory department.

   f) Describe how laboratory testing is used to assess body functions and disease.

g) Use common medical terminology.

2) Communicate (verbally and nonverbally) effectively and appropriately in the workplace.

   a) Maintain confidentiality of privileged information on individuals.

   b) Value diversity in the workplace.

   c) Interact appropriately and professionally with other individuals.

   d) Model professional appearance and appropriate behavior.

Medical Law and Ethics

This is a course of instruction in principles, procedures, and regulations involving legal and ethical relationships among physicians, patients, and medical assistants. It includes current ethical issues as they relate to the practice of medicine and conformity responsibilities.

LEARNING OBJECTIVES

   a. Define ethics, bioethics, and law

   b. Discuss the measures a medical practice must take to avoid malpractice claims

   a. Discuss the major points of the American Hospital Associations' Patient's Bill of Rights or the Patient's Bill of Rights from the institution.

   b. Define the different terms used in the Medicolegal aspect for phlebotomy and discuss policies and protocol designed to avoid Medicolegal problems.

   c. Follow written and verbal instructions in carrying out testing procedures.

d. List the causes of stress in the work environment and discuss the coping skills used to deal with stress in the work environment.

e. Demonstrate ability to use computer information systems necessary to accomplish job functions.

Anatomy, Physiology, Medical Terminology

The overall objective of the program is to acquire knowledge of the anatomy and physiology of the human body. Includes an overview of the diseases related to each anatomical system. Functional concepts and internal structure are related as a basis for performing a physical examination. Course also includes an understanding of the language of medicine.

LEARNING OBJECTIVES: Demonstrate basic understanding of the anatomy and physiology of body systems and anatomic terminology in order to relate major areas of the clinical laboratory to general pathologic conditions associated with the body systems.

a. Describe the basic functions of each of the main body systems, and demonstrate basic knowledge of the circulatory, urinary, and other body systems necessary to perform assigned specimen collection tasks.

b. Identify the veins of the arms, hands, legs and feet on which phlebotomy is performed.

c. Explain the functions of the major constituents of blood, and differentiate between whole blood, serum and plasma.

d. Define hemostasis, and explain the basic process of coagulation

e.   Discuss the properties of arterial blood, venous blood, and capillary blood.

Asepsis and Infection Control

A study of standard protocol for the protection of the healthcare worker and patient to ensure that the procedures and treatments prescribed by the physician are safely and properly performed to assist the patient's return to health. Overview of causes and prevention of chain of infection.

LEARNING OBJECTIVES: Demonstrate knowledge of infection control and safety.

a.   Identify policies and procedures for maintaining laboratory safety.

b.   Demonstrate accepted practices for infection control, isolation techniques, aseptic techniques and methods for disease prevention.

c.   Identify and discuss the modes of transmission of infection and methods for prevention.

d.   Identify and properly label biohazardous specimens.

e.   Discuss in detail and perform proper infection control techniques, such as handwashing, gowning, gloving, masking, and double-bagging.

f.   Define and discuss the term "nosocomial infection".

g.   Comply with federal, state and locally mandated regulations regarding safety practices.

h.   Use the OSHA Standard Precautions

i. Use prescribed procedures to handle electrical, radiation, biological and fire hazards.

j. Use appropriate practices, as outlined in the OSHA Hazard Communications Standard, including the correct use of the Material Safety Data Sheet as directed.

k. Describe measures used to insure patient safety in various patient settings, i.e., inpatient, outpatient, pediatrics, etc.

CPR and First Aid

The focus of this course will provide a general understanding the needs of the injured person and, in doing so, give care to the person including CPR until medical help is obtained. This module aims to illustrate emergency situations that may arise in a Phlebotomists daily routine and the response techniques learners will require to intervene appropriately during such circumstances. This course is not intended as a certification course for CPR. However, some training institutions require that students obtain their CPR/First Aid training before enrolling into their program. In such cases, they may not repeat this course in the program.

LEARNING OBJECTIVES

1. Explain the purpose and value of first aid and CPR training.

2. List the roles and responsibilities of the citizen responder and professional rescuer.

3. Explain Emergency Action Plans; First Aid: wounds, shock, special injuries sudden illness; poisoning; heat/cold emergencies; special situations that may occur during venipuncture/arterial/capillary collections.

4. List the symptoms of latex allergy and explain the appropriate action plan.

5. Demonstrate rescue breathing techniques for adult, child, and infant.

6. Demonstrate proper CPR techniques for adult, child, and infant including two-person adult.

7. Explain the Automated External Defibrillator and its use.

8. Describe appropriate first aid care for shock

9. Describe appropriate immediate first aid care for complications during phlebotomy procedures.

10. Describe appropriate first aid care for sudden illnesses.

11. Express the ability to analyze and evaluate various emergency care situations.

12. Demonstrates self-confidence during practical testing of skills.

Venipuncture

This course is designed to instruct the student in the proper methods of both capillary and Venus blood collection. Equipment, legal issues and specimen transport are taught and practiced. Proper methods of blood collections and processing are taught and practiced.

LEARNING OBJECTIVES

1) Demonstrate understanding of the importance of specimen collection and specimen integrity in the delivery of patient care.

   a) Describe the legal and ethical importance of proper patient/sample identification.

   b) Describe the types of patient specimens that are analyzed in the clinical laboratory.

   c) Define the phlebotomist's role in collecting and/or transporting these specimens to the laboratory.

   d) List the general criteria for suitability of a specimen for analysis, and reasons for specimen rejection or recollection.

   e) Explain the importance of timed, fasting and stat specimens, as related to specimen integrity and patient care.

2) Demonstrate knowledge of collection equipment, various types of additives used, special precautions necessary and substances that can interfere in clinical analysis of blood constituents.

   a) Identify the various types of additives used in blood collection, and explain the reasons for their use.

   b) Identify the evacuated tube color codes associated with the additives.

   c) Describe substances that can interfere in clinical analysis of blood constituents and ways in which the phlebotomist can help to avoid these occurrences.

   d) List and select the types of equipment needed to collect blood by venipuncture, capillary, and arterial puncture.

   e) Identify special precautions necessary during blood collections by venipuncture, capillary, and arterial puncture.

3) Follow standard operating procedures to collect specimens.

   a) Identify potential sites for venipuncture, capillary, and arterial punctures.

   b) Differentiate between sterile and antiseptic techniques.

   c) Describe and demonstrate the steps in the preparation of a puncture site.

   d) List the effect of tourniquet, hand squeezing and heating pads on capillary puncture and venipuncture.

   e) Recognize proper needle insertion and withdrawal techniques including direction, angle, depth and aspiration, for arterial puncture and venipuncture.

   f) Describe and perform correct procedure for capillary collection methods on infants and adults.

g) Identify alternate collection sites for arterial, capillary and venipuncture. Describe the limitations and precautions of each.

h) Name and explain frequent causes of phlebotomy complications. Describe signs and symptoms of physical problems that may occur during blood collection.

i) List the steps necessary to perform an arterial, venipuncture and/or capillary puncture in chronological order.

j) Follow standard operating procedures to perform a competent/effective venipuncture on a patient.

k) Follow standard operating procedures to perform a competent/effective capillary puncture on a patient.

4) Demonstrate understanding of requisitioning, specimen transport and specimen processing.

a) Describe the standard operating procedure for a physician requesting a laboratory analysis for a patient. Discuss laboratory responsibility in responding to physician requests.

b) Instruct patients in the proper collection and preservation for various samples, including blood, sputum, and stools.

c) Explain methods for transporting and processing specimens for routine and special testing.

d) Explain methods for processing and transporting blood specimens for testing at reference laboratories.

e) Describe the potential clerical and technical errors that may occur during specimen processing.

f) Identify and report potential pre-analytical errors that may occur during specimen collection, labeling, transporting, and processing.

g) Describe and follow the criteria for specimens and test results that will be used as legal evidence, i.e. paternity testing, chain of custody, blood alcohol levels, etc.

5) Demonstrate understanding of quality assurance and quality control in phlebotomy.

a) Describe the system for monitoring quality assurance in the collection of blood specimens.

b) Identify policies and procedures used in the clinical laboratory to assure quality in the obtaining of blood specimens.

c) Perform quality control procedures.

d) Record quality control results.

e) Identify and report control results that do not meet pre-determined criteria.

Career Development

This course is designed to assist the student in resume development, interviewing strategies and decision-making skills to assist the student in obtaining employment. Optional externships are encouraged to offer the student the opportunity for real-life experience and additional 'on-the-job' training.

PERFORMANCE OBJECTIVES: At the conclusion of this course, student will:

1. Present an acceptable resume using an industry recognized format.

2. Present an acceptable cover letter and/or fax cover sheet using an industry recognized format.

3. Present themselves in a professional manner for interviews.

4. Understand the roles of the interviewer and the interviewee.

5. Demonstrate appropriate interview behavior

6. Demonstrate the ability to review and respond to appropriate help wanted ads in the newspaper

7. Demonstrate ability to conduct an Internet search for jobs within their field.
8. Present a written 'thank you' note for interviewer.

CERTIFIED PATIENT CARE TECHNICIAN

SIGNIFICANT POINTS:

- Some patient care technicians are trained on the job, but many complete a minimum of 200 hour instruction in schools, community or junior colleges.

- Job prospects should be best for patient care technicians with formal training or experience, particularly those with certification.

NATURE OF THE WORK

Patient Care Technicians, also known as nursing assistants, geriatric aides, unlicensed assistive personnel, or hospital attendants, perform routine tasks under the supervision of nursing and medical staff. They answer patients' call lights, deliver messages, serve meals, make beds, and help patients eat, dress, and bathe. Aides also may provide skin care to patients; take their temperatures, pulse rate, respiration rate, and blood pressure; and help patients get in and out of bed and walk. They also may escort patients to operating and examining rooms, keep patients' rooms neat, set up equipment, store and move supplies, or assist with some procedures. Aides observe patients' physical, mental, and emotional conditions and report any change to the nursing or medical staff.

Nursing and psychiatric aides help care for physically or mentally ill, injured, disabled, or infirm individuals confined to hospitals, nursing care facilities, and mental health settings. Home health aides' duties are similar, but they work in patients' homes or residential care facilities.

Home health aides help elderly, convalescent, or disabled persons live in their own homes instead of in a health facility. Under the direction of nursing or medical staff, they provide health-related services, such as administering oral medications. Personal and home care aides are individuals who provide mainly housekeeping and routine personal care services. Like nursing aides, home health aides may check patients' pulse rates, temperatures, and respiration rates; help with simple prescribed exercises; keep patients' rooms neat; and help patients move from bed, bathe, dress, and groom. Occasionally, they change non-sterile dressings, give massages and alcohol rubs, or assist with braces and artificial limbs. Experienced home health aides also may assist with medical equipment such as ventilators, which help patients breathe. When preparing for the national certifying exam for patient care technicians, I would highly recommend my book: **Patient Care Technician Certification Exam Review Questions**. It is available on www.bestamericanhealthed.com/resources.html

Some states would allow patient care technicians to work as home health aides while some states like California would require a specific certification as a home health aide. Check your state policies.

WORKING CONDITIONS

Most full-time patient care technicians work about 40 hours a week. However, since some patients need care 24 hours a day, some PCTs work evenings, nights, weekends, and holidays. Many work part time. PCTs spend many hours standing and walking, and they often face heavy workloads. Because they may have to move patients in and out of bed or help them stand or walk, aides must guard against back injury. PCTs also may face hazards from minor infections and major diseases, such as hepatitis, but can avoid infections by following proper procedures.

PCTs often have unpleasant duties, such as emptying bedpans and changing soiled bed linens. The patients they care for may be disoriented, irritable, or uncooperative. While their work can be emotionally demanding, many PCTs gain satisfaction from assisting those in need.

EMPLOYMENT

Some employers provide classroom instruction for newly hired PCTs, while others rely exclusively on informal on-the-job instruction from a licensed nurse or an experienced tech. Such training may last several days to a few months. From time to time, PCTs also may attend lectures, workshops, and in-service training.

These occupations can offer individuals an entry into the world of work. The flexibility of night and weekend hours also provides high school and college students a chance to work during the school year.

Applicants should be tactful, patient, understanding, emotionally stable, and dependable and should have a desire to help people. They also should be able to work as part of a team, have good communication skills, and be willing to perform repetitive, routine tasks.

PCTs must be in good health. A physical examination, including State-regulated tests such as those for tuberculosis, may be required.

JOB OUTLOOK

Numerous job openings for patient care technicians will arise from a combination of fast employment growth and high replacement needs. High replacement needs in this large occupation reflect modest entry requirements, low pay, high physical and emotional demands, and lack of opportunities for advancement. For these same reasons, many people are unwilling to perform the kind of work required by the occupation. Therefore, persons who are interested in, and suited for, this work should have excellent job opportunities.

Overall employment of patient care technicians is projected to grow for all occupations through the year 2020, although individual occupational growth rates will vary. Employment of PCTs is expected to grow the fastest, as a result of both growing demand for home healthcare services from an aging population and efforts to contain healthcare costs by moving patients out of hospitals and nursing care facilities as quickly as possible. Consumer preference for care in the home and improvements in medical technologies for in-home treatment also will contribute to faster-than-average employment growth for PCTs.

DESCRIPTION:

This program will prepare the student for an entry-level position as a patient care technician. Emphasis is on technical skills necessary to perform personal care to complex patients, implementation of selected portions of care plans, including respiratory services, rehabilitation services, EKG and phlebotomy under the supervision of registered nurses.

This is a competency-based curriculum; therefore there are institutional differences on the minimum hours. The recommended minimum is 200 hours. The curriculum for the Patient Care Technician usually includes:

Introduction to Patient Care

Students learn to perform a variety of acute-care skills related to the hospital setting. The needs of adult patients with specific health problems such as diabetes, arthritis, spinal cord injuries and seizure disorders among others, are discussed.

Psychological Aspect of Patient Care

This course provides the student with skills important to effective communication as it relates to patient care. Emphasis is placed on the effective verbal, nonverbal, written communication skills. Leadership, teamwork strategies for relating to patients and families should be emphasized.

Medical Anatomy and Physiology

This course is a study of human anatomy and physiology. Lectures systematically take the student from the microscopic level through the formation of organ systems, with emphasis on the interdependence of these systems. Functional concepts and internal structure are related to surface anatomy as a basis for performing a physical examination. The physiology lectures will provide the overall physiology of the human body but will also relate how that physiology breaks down or malfunctions in time of infection, disease, trauma, and aging.

Medical Terminology

This course is a study of a medical vocabulary system. It includes structure, recognition, analysis, definition, spelling, pronunciation, and combination of medical terms from prefixes, suffixes, roots and combining forms.

Medical Law and Ethics

This is a course of instruction in principles, procedures, and regulations involving legal and ethical relationships among physicians, patients, and medical assistants. It includes current ethical issues as they relate to the practice of medicine and conformity responsibilities. This is a writing intensive course.

Asepsis and Infection Control

This course is a study of standard protocol for the protection of the health care worker and patient to ensure that the procedures and treatments prescribed by the physician are performed properly and safely to assist in the patients return to health.

CPR and First Aid

This course will cover the theory and practical skills of the standard first aid course prescribed by the American Red Cross, American Heart Association or other national certification bodies. The focus of this course will provide a general understanding of the needs of the injured person and, in doing so, give care to the person including CPR until medical help is obtained.

Ambulatory

This course is a study that focuses on clinical skills performed by the patient care technician in the back office of a general medical practice. Students will learn about the concepts of professionalism, communication and triage, patient history, physical assessment, equipment and diagnostic procedures used during the examination to assist the health care provider with diagnosis and perform appropriate charting for medical record documentation.

Basic Nursing Assisting and Geriatric Patient Care

A variety of Nursing Assistant skills are provided. The student learns to perform basic nursing procedures, caring for the patients emotional and physical needs. Principles of Universal Precautions, isolation and infection control are included. Geriatric care is emphasized together with restorative activities and patient care plans.

Home Health Care

Students are introduced to the roles and responsibilities of the home health aide. Topics include legal and ethical responsibilities, patient safety, and physical comfort, nutrition, infection control and communication. Students also learn to follow work plans with the patient and family.

Applied Health Applications

Students perform diverse patient care skills involving allied health modalities within the scope of practice of unlicensed assistive personnel. Basic respiratory care modalities are introduced. Students also learn to perform colostomy care, skin and decubitus care, removal and care of peripheral intravenous catheters, as well as assisting with orthopedic devices.

Introduction to EKG

This course introduces students to patient preparation, EKG machines, performing and mounting of 12 lead, single channel EKG tracings. Review of the cardiovascular system and related terminology. Emphasis on basic rhythm identification and possible disease states.

Applied EKG

Advanced knowledge of the cardiovascular system with emphasis on the heart in disease states including identification of cardiac arrhythmias using EKG wave form, interpretation of advanced arrhythmias, hypertrophies, cardiac ischemia, and myocardial infarction is discussed.

Clinical EKG

This course provides advanced training which is often required to obtain employment in the field; cardiac stress testing, artificial pacemaker evaluation, 24 hour Holter monitoring and advanced cardiac arrhythmia recognition and telemetry monitoring. Students use equipment which includes the pacemaker simulator, Holter monitor recorders, 3-channel EKG recording systems and telemetry monitors.

Introduction to Phlebotomy

Introduction course that explains the function of today's Phlebotomy Technicians such as collection procedures, therapeutic phlebotomy and laboratory testing.

Hematology

This is a basic hematology course that studies the cells of the blood. Time is spent learning the technique to enumerate blood cells, understand the function of each cell and to learn the diseases or conditions that would result in abnormalities in the laboratory tests performed. Techniques in making and staining a blood smear along with evaluation and differentiation of the blood cell through microscopic examination. Proper methods of blood collections and processing are taught and practiced

Applied Venipuncture

This course is designed to instruct the student in the proper methods of both capillary and venous blood collection. Equipment, legal issues and specimen transport and taught and practiced.

Clinical Phlebotomy

Clinical phlebotomy expands the skills and experiences at a clinic and/or hospital setting under the direct supervision of a medical laboratory technician or technologist. The student will comprehend and follow procedural guidelines for laboratory testing including specimen collection, specimen processing, result reporting, and record documentation. Quality assurance monitoring in the collection of blood, complying with safety requirements, and professionalism with patients, coworkers, and healthcare professionals are also emphasized.

HIPAA Compliance

This is a short course of study that discusses the patient's right to privacy, the laws and regulations of the Health Insurance Portability and Accountability Act (HIPAA). The governing bodies that set these standards and penalties provided for non-compliance are also discussed.

Externship

Students are placed in a medical facility where there is an opportunity to observe, assist, learn, and perform patient services in an acute care setting. The externship is an essential component of the program where theoretical and practical skills are integrated. Specific objectives, including cognitive, affective, and psychomotor behaviors must be met for students to complete this course.

Career Development

This course is designed to assist the student in resume development, soft skills, interviewing strategies and decision-making skills to assist the student in obtaining employment. Optional externships are encouraged to offer the student the opportunity for real-life experience.

At the end of the course module, the student should:

- List the composition of Cells, Tissues, Organs and Systems

- Describe the correlation between cells and systems

- Identify the organs within each system and their function

- Identify and utilize the correct root word for each organ

- Explain the importance of controlling the spread of infectious organisms

- Identify the meaning of Infection, Microorganism, and Pathogen

- List the chain of infection

- Explain Universal Precautions

- Identify proper hand washing techniques as the most important step in Infection Control

- Differentiate isolation techniques and the purpose of their use

- List the equipment needed to perform a Phlebotomy procedure

- Use proper venipuncture cleansing technique

- Use a tourniquet and explain the purpose of its use

- Differentiate the two methods of draw

- List the order of draw for each method

- Identify the different needles used in Phlebotomy

- Understand the difference in the needle gauges

- Use the proper needle gauge and type for the procedure

- Differentiate the different color tubes used in phlebotomy

- Explain the purpose of the additives in the tubes

- Identify the tests, which can be taken in the presence of such additives

- Determine which color tubes to use for the tests ordered

- Identify the various special testing the technician may perform

- Explain why these tests are important in the diagnosing of diseases

- Identify normal ranges and abnormal results

- Perform the various tests and related procedures

- Recognize phlebotomy-related complications

- Identify possible life threatening complications

- Act upon the specific complication

- Properly notify Nursing personnel regarding such complication

- Discuss the various departments within the laboratory

- Explain the laboratory hierarchy, and the different personnel titles and job related duties

- Identify the collection schedules within the healthcare setting

- Differentiate the duties of the pct within a blood collection bank

- Utilize the phlebotomy equipment ensuring patient safety, and employee safety

- Follow infection control procedure

- Observe universal precaution

- Obtain blood from the manikin

- Perform all of the tests utilizing proper technique

- List the procedures for electrocardiography

- Define Electrodes, Electrocardiograph, Electrocardiography, Electrolyte Gel

- Properly place the electrodes

- Perform a 12 lead EKG

- Connect Holter Monitors

- Perform Stress Tests

- Understand Angiocardiographic studies, Cardiac Catherization

- Use the proper Medical Terminology associated with EKG testing

- List the characteristics needed to be a successful member of the healthcare team

- List the duties of a Patient Care Associate/Technician

- Explain how interpersonal relations influence the well-being of the patient

- Describe the purpose of the interdisciplinary team

- Demonstrate professional attitude

- List ergonomic techniques, which can prevent incidents

- Demonstrate the correct use of body mechanics

- Use equipment safely

- Describe the proper use of oxygen and related safety

- Identify proper fire safety techniques

- Follow proper evacuation procedure guidelines

- List general measures to take in the event of an emergency

- Recognize the emergency situations

- Explain the purpose of the patient's bill of rights

- Follow the rule of personal liability

- Discuss and interpret informed consent

- Observe DNR orders

- Describe the legalities involving the patient's medical record

- Observe patient confidentiality

- Describe the laws pertaining to medicine

- Discuss quality assurance procedures

- Communicate with the patient, family members and staff

- Use the communication process

- Be aware of the body language being used

- Discuss the proper tone to use when communicating in different scenarios

- Receive, record proper phone messages

- Make subjective/ objective observation

- The student will demonstrate understanding of the theory of Patient Care Technician by scoring a minimum of 70% on the National Certification written exam.

Certified Medical Administrative Assistant

Upon completion of the course, the student should be able to:
- Articulate the main roles and responsibilities of the Medical Office Assistant, including administrative, clinical and general.
- Identify different types of medical institutions and medical offices.
- Understand personal/professional, medical/legal and bio-ethical standards, and the importance of safeguarding confidentiality.
- Define acceptable office behavior, including proper telephone etiquette and the importance of patient sensitivity and confidentiality.
- Define medical malpractice, abandonment, fraud and abuse
- Be able to distinguish among the five drug schedules of controlled substances
- List procedures for scheduling and referring patients, and handling walk-in emergency patients
- Identify and discuss at least three important interpersonal skills

- Identify and become familiar with the various types of written correspondence in a medical office
- Create a block-style letter that conforms to all formatting requirements
- Understand what is required to create and submit a medical bill.
- Define a Release of Medical Information, Explanation of Benefit, Assignment of Benefit, and Electronic Remittance Advice
- Develop an understanding of the term HMO, and be able to interpret the information contained on the patient's insurance card
- Define the terms and distinguish among: Express, Implied and Informed Consents
- Understand the financial terms and procedures involved in operating a medical office practice, including Income, Expense, Accounts Receivable, Accounts Payable, Cash and Accrual Accounting, Write-off Adjustments
- Define safety and infection control standards and procedures in a medical office
- Demonstrate awareness of HIPAA Compliance, Confidentiality Laws, PHI
- Create a personal Resume and Cover Letter incorporating the new medical office skills and concepts developed through this course

DESCRIPTION:

This course prepares students for the administrative skills medical administrative assistants need to know. This program integrates all of the front office topics and skill competencies required for today's industry standards. This program also covers material dealing with medical office, medical records, management skills, client service skills and responsibilities, client education and legal/ethical issues.

COURSE PREREQUISITE(S):   none.

METHOD OF INSTRUCTION: This course utilizes a lecture and demonstration methodology.

This course covers the following topics:

Introduction to Healthcare:

This is an introductory course that explores the roles and responsibilities associated with today's medical office environment. Various medical specialties of allied healthcare workers, physician specialties and hospitals will be explored. Students will gain an understanding of the hospital environment, the physician office, clinics, and other medical facilities.

Introduction to Health Insurance

Introductory course that gives an overview of the insurance industry. Concepts such as: What is Health Insurance? Disability and Liability Insurance; Major Developments in Health Insurance; and Third Party Reimbursement Methods. This is a course designed to introduce the students to the medical insurance claims process. Students will learn: Developments of the Claim, Insurance Company Processing of a Claim and Maintaining Insurance Claim Files. (This course is an introduction to the Health Insurance Process and is not intended to satisfy requirements for the Certified Billing & Coding Specialist program. Students are not eligible for the CBCS Certification.)

Medical Terminology

This course introduces students to medical terminology and includes an overview of anatomy and physiology, medical history, examination procedures, and medical reports. The course also covers terminology related to diseases, diagnostic tests, and treatment of body systems. Students will also learn terminology related to radiology, pathology, autopsies, mental health, and discharge summaries.

OBJECTIVES: Upon successful completion of the course, student will:

1. Begin developing a medical vocabulary through a study of root words

2. Begin developing a medical vocabulary through a study of prefixes and suffixes

3. Students will develop practices of correct pronunciation and usage of terms

4. Students will develop an understanding related to the following body systems:

   a. Integumentary,

   b. musculoskeletal,

   c. circulatory,

   d. lymphatic,

   e. cardiovascular,

   f. respiratory,

   g. digestive,

   h. urinary,

   i. reproductive,

   j. endocrine,

k. nervous,

l. Senses (eye, ear and throat)

Medical Laws and Ethics:

This course examines the role of the Certified Medical Administrative Assistant and the laws that relate to this role. Special emphasis on OSHA regulations relating to the front office; HIPAA Compliance; Employer and Employee Liability; Patients' Bill of Rights; Americans with Disabilities Act; and Fraud.

OBJECTIVES: Upon successful completion of this course, the student will:

1. Define roles and responsibilities related to the Certified Medical Administrative Assistant (CMAA).

2. Discuss the principles of medical ethics as they apply to both the CMAA and the physician

3. Discuss the Patients Bill of Rights and responsibilities in receiving medical care

4. Demonstrate understanding of HIPAA Compliance and Person Health Information, PHI.

5. Demonstrate understanding of OSHA regulations

6. Demonstrate understanding of the American's with Disabilities Act

7. Demonstrate understanding of Employee/Employer Liability

Introduction to Computers.

This course is designed to familiarize the student with primary computer skills. Students will begin with the key components (hardware) of the computer. This course will start with the fundamentals of the computer system and advance to the basics of the software of the computer. Students will learn fundamentals of computer software, storage systems, back-up systems, Internet/Intranet and the concepts of computer networks.

OBJECTIVES: Upon completion of this course, the student will:

1. Properly identify the key components of the computer

2. Demonstrate ability to turn the computer on and off correctly

3. Demonstrate ability to use the mouse correctly

4. Demonstrate the ability to turn the monitor on and off correctly

5. Demonstrate the ability to turn the printer on and off

6. Describe a modem and its function

7. Correctly label the parts of the computer: cd rom; floppy disk and explain their use.

8. Explain the terms: Operating system, application programs and software compatibility

9. Explain computer networks, electronic mail and the Internet

10. Explain professional behavior regarding the Internet

11. Explain professional behavior and security regarding computers

Business Writing and Communication.

This course is designed to introduce the student to basic concepts and skills for the office environment. Students will learn the principles of written communications needed to communicate effectively in a medical environment by composing business letters, memos and reports. Students will develop proof reading skills; review grammar, spelling and vocabulary. .

OBJECTIVES: Upon successful completion of this course, the student will:

1. Demonstrate understanding of the format of a business letter.

2. Demonstrate the ability to create a business letter in two formats.

3. Students will demonstrate the ability of using reference books such as a dictionary and a thesaurus.

4. Students will demonstrate understanding of rules of grammar.

5. Students will demonstrate understanding of spelling rules and improve spelling

6. Students will demonstrate improved vocabulary.

7. Demonstrate understanding of proof-reading, editing and corrections.

8. Students will develop understanding of proof-readers marks.

9. Students will improve proof reading skills.

10. Students will demonstrate the ability to proofread and edit a report.

Medical Keyboarding.

This course is designed to teach the student keyboarding skills via the computer. Students will learn the typing skills necessary to learn the alpha and numeric keyboards. Students will utilize drill practice to gain speed and accuracy. Emphasis will be placed on medical reports, terminology and other types of documentation essential in a medical office environment.

OBJECTIVES: Upon completion of this course, the student will:

1. Define the parts of functions of the computer keyboard

2. Demonstrate the understanding of function keys, space bar, enter and letter keys

3. Demonstrate proper finger and hand placement on keyboard

4. Utilize all 10 fingers while typing.

5. The student will be able to demonstrate ability to type without looking at keyboard at a speed of 20 wpm with no more than three errors.

6. The student will demonstrate understanding of the numeric keypad.

7. The student will demonstrate ability to create a business letter in two formats.

8. The student will demonstrate ability to create a letter of collection.

9. The student will demonstrate the ability to create an invoice for collection using tab numbers.

Fundamentals of Mathematics.

Students will review basic math topics and common applications for the medical office

1. Students will demonstrate ability to perform simple mathematic functions: addition, subtraction, multiplication and division.

2. Students will demonstrate ability to perform simple mathematic functions of addition and subtractions of decimals..

3. Demonstrate ability to solve word problems involving decimals and percentages

4. Demonstrate ability to solve numeric and word problems involving common situations in the medical office.

Accounting and Finance for the Medical Office.

This course is designed to introduce bookkeeping and basic accounting skills needed in a medical office practice. Students will learn about banking services and procedures. The emphasis of this hands-on office simulation is accuracy and confidentiality of medical office records. The student will assume the role of the medical office professional and will be learning various tasks required in posting and tabulating patient financial records.

Computer Applications.

This course is designed to provide students with a basic understanding of a window-based environment and word processing using Microsoft word. Students will learn to create, edit, retrieve and produce documents via various hands-on applications. Students will also be introduced to spreadsheet concepts using Microsoft Excel applications. Students will be given an opportunity to improve speed and accuracy on the computer keyboard.

OBJECTIVES: Upon successful completion, the student will:

1. Be able to create, edit and print a document.

2. Demonstrate ability to format, set margins and set tabs on a document.

3. Demonstrate ability to move/copy text and find/replace text.

4. Demonstrate ability to open and edit documents and manage files

5. Demonstrate ability to create a document utilizing different fonts within the document.

6. Demonstrate the ability to create a basic spreadsheet

7. Demonstrate understanding of formulas and formatting data

8. Demonstrate ability to print selections from spreadsheets

9. Demonstrate ability to change fonts, colors and patterns and cell borders

10. Demonstrate ability to create, name and edit spreadsheets

11. Demonstrate ability to enter data utilizing only numeric pad

Customer Service for the Healthcare Professional.

This course is the study of effective patient relations and the skills that need to be mastered to provide quality customer service to patients and other healthcare workers. Students will learn professionalism needed speak to patients and other healthcare workers and will develop mastery of appropriate behaviors needed for the medical office. Students will learn telephone skills; answering calls; messages; and how to handle irate patients. Special emphasis will be placed on cultural differences; oral communications (effective speaking); verbal and non-verbal communications; teamwork with co-workers; soft-skills.

OBJECTIVES: Upon successful completion of this course, the student will:

1. Demonstrate understanding of verbal and non-verbal communication

2. Demonstrate appropriate telephone techniques

3. Demonstrate message taking by creating messages

4. Demonstrate ability to handle various customer calls

5. Demonstrate understanding of "ACTIVE LISTENING"

6. Demonstrate ability to manage a multi-line phone

7. Demonstrate appropriate HIPAA protocols when answering questions

8. Demonstrate understanding of cultural differences among various groups

9. Demonstrate understanding the roles of the CMAA and other healthcare professionals

10. Demonstrate the ability to assist special needs customers

Medical Office Skills I:

This course is designed to teach the student the protocols of New Patient Interview and Check-in Procedure; Established Patient Return Visit; Post Clinical Check-out Procedure. Students will gain an understanding of concepts such as pre-authorization, and the 'smart card'. Students will learn how to schedule appointments, record management, preparing medical records. Students will learn how to arrange medical meetings and travel arrangements.

Medical Documentation

Students will gain a thorough understanding of the medical documentation process. Students will learn the guidelines for documentation, medical records, and laws governing privacy of medical documents. Students will learn how to prepare medical reports in the proper format, interpretation of medical chart. Concentration: medical office workflow, medical record management, correspondence, communications.

OBJECTIVES: Upon completion of this course, students will:

1. Discuss parts of the medical record

2. Demonstrate the ability to create a new chart

3. Demonstrate the ability to file medical records using various filing formats

4. differentiate between new patient, established patient and follow-up

5. define new patient emergency visit; established patient emergency visit, emergency situations

6. Discuss history and physical. (Styles and formats)

7. Identify physical exam data

8. Demonstrate how to enter data correctly onto a patient chart

9. Differentiate between the various types of medical reports transcribed

10. Identify the format needed for each of the medical reports

11. interpret a chart and prepare the medical report

12. Create reports: Discharge Summary; Operative Reports; Consultation Report; Medicolegal Reports

Career Development. This optional course will prepare the students to identify and evaluate career opportunities, locate potential employers and prepare for job interviews.

OBJECTIVES: At the conclusion of this course, student will:

9. Present an acceptable resume

10. Present an acceptable cover letter and/or fax cover sheet.

11. Present themselves in a professional manner for interviews.

12. Understand the roles of the interviewer and the interviewee.

13. Demonstrate appropriate interview behavior

14. Demonstrate the ability to review and respond to appropriate help wanted ads in the newspaper

15. Demonstrate ability to conduct an Internet search for jobs within their field.

16. Present a 'thank you' note written for interviewer.

Clinical Medical Assisting

Medical assistants work primarily in ambulatory settings such as medical offices and clinics. Medical assistants function as members of the healthcare delivery team and may perform administrative and/or clinical procedures. Administrative duties include scheduling and receiving patients, preparing and maintaining medical records, performing basic secretarial skills and medical transcription, handling telephone calls and writing correspondence, serving as a liaison between the physician and other individuals, and managing practice finances.

DUTIES:

A. Display Professionalism

B. Apply Communication Skills

C. Demonstrate Keyboarding Skills And Computer Awareness

D. Perform Business Software Applications

E. Work Within Computer Operating Environments

F. Perform Administrative Duties

G. Apply Legal, Ethical, And Confidentiality Concepts To Practice

H. Manage The Office

I. Provide Patient Instruction

J. Manage Practice Finances

DESCRIPTION:

This program is designed to teach students the skills necessary for employment in the modern medical facility. A qualified medical assistant is capable of performing a wide range of duties, with a variety of technical detail; thus helping the physician in many clinical situations. Upon successful completion of this course, students sit for a national certification exam.

SIGNIFICANT POINTS

- Some medical assistants are trained on the job, but many complete 1- or 2-year programs in vocational-technical high schools, postsecondary vocational schools, and community and junior colleges.

- Medical assisting is projected to be the fastest growing occupation over the past decade

- Job prospects should be best for medical assistants with formal training or experience, particularly those with certification.

NATURE OF THE WORK

Medical assistants perform routine administrative and clinical tasks to keep the offices of physicians, podiatrists, chiropractors, and other health practitioners running smoothly. They should not be confused with physician assistants, who examine, diagnose, and treat patients under the direct supervision of a physician. The duties of medical assistants vary from office to office, depending on the location and size of the practice and the practitioner's specialty. In small practices, medical assistants usually are "generalists," handling both administrative and clinical duties and reporting directly to an office manager, physician, or other health practitioner. Those in large practices tend to specialize in a particular area, under the supervision of department administrators.

Medical assistants perform many administrative duties, including answering telephones, greeting patients, updating and filing patients' medical records, filling out insurance forms, handling correspondence, scheduling appointments, arranging for hospital admission and laboratory services, and handling billing and bookkeeping.

Clinical duties vary according to State law and include taking medical histories and recording vital signs, explaining treatment procedures to patients, preparing patients for examination, and assisting the physician during the examination. Medical assistants collect and prepare laboratory specimens or perform basic laboratory tests on the premises, dispose of contaminated supplies, and sterilize medical instruments. They instruct patients about medications and special diets, prepare and administer medications as directed by a physician, authorize drug refills as directed, telephone prescriptions to a pharmacy, draw blood, prepare patients for x rays, take electrocardiograms, remove sutures, and change dressings.

Medical assistants also may arrange examining-room instruments and equipment, purchase and maintain supplies and equipment, and keep waiting and examining rooms neat and clean.

Assistants who specialize have additional duties. *Podiatric medical assistants* make castings of feet, expose and develop x rays, and assist podiatrists in surgery. *Ophthalmic medical assistants* help ophthalmologists provide eye care. They conduct diagnostic tests, measure and record vision, and test eye muscle function. They also show patients how to insert, remove, and care for contact lenses, and they apply eye dressings. Under the direction of the physician, ophthalmic medical assistants may administer eye medications. They also maintain optical and surgical instruments and may assist the ophthalmologist in surgery.

WORKING CONDITIONS

Medical assistants work in well-lighted, clean environments. They constantly interact with other people and may have to handle several responsibilities at once.

Most full-time medical assistants work a regular 40-hour week. Some work part time, evenings, or weekends.

EMPLOYMENT

Medical assistants held about 365,000 jobs in 2002. Almost 60 percent worked in offices of physicians; about 14 percent worked in public and private hospitals, including inpatient and outpatient facilities; and almost 10 percent worked in offices of other health practitioners, such as chiropractors and podiatrists. The rest worked mostly in outpatient care centers, public and private educational services, other ambulatory healthcare services, State and local government agencies, medical and diagnostic laboratories, nursing care facilities, and employment services.

TRAINING, OTHER QUALIFICATIONS, AND ADVANCEMENT

Most employers prefer graduates of formal programs in medical assisting. Such programs are offered in vocational-technical high schools, postsecondary vocational schools, and community and junior colleges. Postsecondary programs usually last either 6 months,1 year, resulting in a certificate or diploma, or 2 years, resulting in an associate degree. Courses cover anatomy, physiology, and medical terminology, as well as typing, transcription, recordkeeping, accounting, and insurance processing. Students learn laboratory techniques, clinical and diagnostic procedures, pharmaceutical principles, the administration of medications, and first aid. They study office practices, patient relations, medical law, and ethics. Accredited programs include an internship that provides practical experience in physicians' offices, hospitals, or other healthcare facilities.

Formal training in medical assisting, while generally preferred, is not always required. Some medical assistants are trained on the job, although this practice is less common than in the past. Applicants usually need a high school diploma or the equivalent. Recommended high school courses include mathematics, health, biology, typing, bookkeeping, computers, and office skills. Volunteer experience in the healthcare field also is helpful.

Although medical assistants are not licensed, some States require them to take a test or a course before they can perform certain tasks, such as taking x rays. Employers prefer to hire experienced workers or certified applicants who have passed a national examination, indicating that the medical assistant meets certain standards of competence. The American Association of Medical Assistants, National Healthcareer Association, and other certifying bodies award the Certified Medical Assistant credential; the American Medical Technologists awards the Registered Medical Assistant credential; the American Society of Podiatric Medical Assistants awards the Podiatric Medical Assistant Certified credential; and the Joint Commission on Allied Health Personnel in Ophthalmology awards credentials at three levels: Certified Ophthalmic Assistant, Certified Ophthalmic Technician, and Certified Ophthalmic Medical Technologist.

Medical assistants deal with the public; therefore, they must be neat and well groomed and have a courteous, pleasant manner. Medical assistants must be able to put patients at ease and explain physicians' instructions. They must respect the confidential nature of medical information. Clinical duties require a reasonable level of manual dexterity and visual acuity.

Medical assistants may be able to advance to office manager. They may qualify for a variety of administrative support occupations or may teach medical assisting. With additional education, some enter other health occupations, such as nursing and medical technology.

JOB OUTLOOK

Employment of medical assistants is expected to grow much faster than the average for all occupations through the year 2020 as the health services industry expands because of technological advances in medicine, and a growing and aging population. Increasing utilization of medical assistants in the rapidly-growing healthcare industries will result in fast employment growth for the occupation.

Employment growth will be driven by the increase in the number of group practices, clinics, and other healthcare facilities that need a high proportion of support personnel, particularly the flexible medical assistant who can handle both administrative and clinical duties. Medical assistants work primarily in outpatient settings, which are expected to exhibit much faster-than-average growth.

In view of the preference of many healthcare employers for trained personnel, job prospects should be best for medical assistants with formal training or experience, and particularly for those with certification.

THE COURSE COVERS THE FOLLOWING TOPICS:

Fundamentals of Medical Assisting

This is an introductory course for the Medical Assistant program. This course places emphasis on patient-centered assessment, examination, intervention and treatment as directed by a physician. It includes vital signs, collection and documentation of patient information, asepsis, minor surgical procedures and other treatments appropriate for the medical office. Medical office procedures and customer service will be discussed. Administrative and clinical competencies are presented. Students will be required to demonstrate proficiency in these skills.

Psychological Aspect of Patient Care

This course provides the student with skills important to effective communication as it relates to patient care. Emphasis is placed on the effective verbal, nonverbal, written communication skills. Leadership, teamwork strategies for relating to patients and families should be emphasized.

Medical Anatomy and Physiology

This course is a study of human anatomy and physiology. Lectures systematically take the student from the microscopic level through the formation of organ systems, with emphasis on the interdependence of these systems. Functional concepts and internal structure are related to surface anatomy as a basis for performing a physical examination. The physiology lectures will provide the overall physiology of the human body but will also relate how that physiology breaks down or malfunctions in time of infection, disease, trauma, and aging.

Medical Terminology

This course is a study of a medical assistant of a medical vocabulary system. It includes structure, recognition, analysis, definition, spelling, pronunciation, and combination of medical terms from prefixes, suffixes, roots and combining forms.

Medical Law and Ethics

This is a course of instruction in principles, procedures, and regulations involving legal and ethical relationships among physicians, patients, and medical assistants. It includes current ethical issues as they relate to the practice of medicine and conformity responsibilities. This is a writing intensive course.

Asepsis and Infection Control

This course is a study of standard protocol for the protection of the health care worker and patient to ensure that the procedures and treatments prescribed by the physician are performed properly and safely to assist in the patients return to health.

CPR and First Aid

This course will cover the theory and practical skills of the standard first aid course prescribed by the American Red Cross, American Heart Association or other certifying bodies. The focus of this course will provide a general understanding the needs of the injured person and, in doing so, give care to the person including CPR until medical help is obtained.

Ambulatory

This course is a study that focuses on clinical skills performed by the medical assistant in the back office of a general medical practice. Students will learn about the concepts of professionalism, communication and triage, patient history, physical assessment, equipment and diagnostic procedures used during the examination to assist the health care provider with diagnosis and perform appropriate charting for medical record documentation.

Introduction and Fundamentals of Pharmacology

This course emphasizes abbreviations and systems of measurement used in administering drug dosages; federal laws in force to control and monitor drug use; and the legal and administrative responsibilities involved in dispensing, administering, and prescribing drugs. This course also covers the forms of medication available for administration and special patient care applications and precautions. Important aspects of patient safety, medication allergies, and patient teaching including pediatric and geriatric populations are studied. Major emphasis is placed on the effects of various drugs on the body systems. Discussion of the most commonly prescribed drugs. Points of emphasis include classes of drugs, actions and uses, side effects, emergency use and patient education.

Introduction to EKG

This course introduces students to patient preparation, EKG machines, performing and mounting of 12 lead, single channel EKG tracings. Review of the cardiovascular system and related terminology. Emphasis on basic rhythm identification and possible disease states.

Applied EKG

Advanced knowledge of the cardiovascular system with emphasis on the heart in disease states including identification of cardiac arrhythmias using EKG wave form, interpretation of advanced arrhythmias, hypertrophies, cardiac ischemia, and myocardial infarction is discussed.

Clinical EKG

This course provides advanced training which is often required to obtain employment in the field; cardiac stress testing, artificial pacemaker evaluation, 24 hour Holter monitoring and advanced cardiac arrhythmia recognition and telemetry monitoring. Students use equipment which includes the pacemaker simulator, Holter monitor recorders, 3-channel EKG recording systems and telemetry monitors.

Introduction to Phlebotomy

Introduction course that explains the function of today's Phlebotomy Technicians such as collection procedures, therapeutic phlebotomy and laboratory testing.

Hematology

This is a basic hematology course that studies the cells of the blood. Time is spent learning the technique to enumerate blood cells, understand the function of each cell and to learn the diseases or conditions that would result in abnormalities in the laboratory tests performed. Techniques in making and staining a blood smear along with evaluation and differentiation of the blood cell through microscopic examination. Proper methods of blood collections and processing are taught and practiced

Applied Venipuncture

This course is designed to instruct the student in the proper methods of both capillary and venous blood collection. Equipment, legal issues and specimen transport and taught and practiced.

Clinical Phlebotomy

The phlebotomy clinical expands the skills and experiences at a clinic and/or hospital setting under the direct supervision of a medical laboratory technician or technologist. The student will comprehend and follow procedural guidelines for laboratory testing including specimen collection, specimen processing, result reporting, and record documentation. Quality assurance monitoring in the collection of blood, complying with safety requirements, and professionalism with patients, coworkers, and healthcare professionals are also emphasized.

The Medical Laboratory

The student is introduced to an area in a healthcare facility where body fluids, cells and tissues are analyzed. Students are introduced to the medical laboratory and its sections delineating each section's setup and function.

Laboratory Quality Assurance/Control

This course explains the importance and need of quality assurance/control in the laboratory with emphasis on the difference between precision and accuracy, use of control when running tests, possible sources of errors and how to minimize them.

Safety in the Medical Laboratory/ Lab Hazards

This course will cover the potential hazards in the medical laboratory: biological, chemical, mechanical, electrical, fire and radiation. Discussed in this course is the importance of following all safety procedures and the incident report as part of the safety program.

The Microscope

The students will know the different parts of a compound microscope, and its various uses in the medical laboratory. The students are taught how to use and care for the compound microscope.

Laboratory Measurements

The students are introduced to the International System of Units: the basic units of measurement for length, mass, and volume. The students are taught how to convert metric units to the English system and vice-versa, and perform basic laboratory measurements.

Urinalysis

This course introduces the purpose of routine urinalysis and its components. Students are taught how to identify proper specimen containers, how to instruct patients to obtain specimen, and proper storage between time of collection and testing.

Clinical Microbiology

The students are taught the main task of the microbiology department: how microorganisms are identified and classified, what types of specimens from the human body are handled and the different types of containers used for transport of the specimens.

HIPAA Compliance

This is a short course of study that discusses the patient's right to privacy, the laws and regulations of the Health Insurance Portability and Accountability Act (HIPAA). The governing bodies that set these standards and penalties provided for non-compliance are also discussed.

Externship

Students are placed in a medical facility where there is an opportunity to observe, assist, learn, and perform patient services in an acute care setting. The externship is an essential component of the program where theoretical and practical skills are integrated. Specific objectives, including cognitive, affective, and psychomotor behaviors must be met for students to complete this course.

Career Development

This course is designed to assist the student in resume development, soft skills, interviewing strategies and decision-making skills to assist the student in obtaining employment. Optional externships are encouraged to offer the student the opportunity for real-life experience.

At the end of the clinical medical assistant module:

- The student will be able to perform hand washing; dispose of bio hazardous materials and practice standard precautions.
- The student will learn how to introduce him or herself in a professional manner.

- The student will be able to perform telephone and in-person screening.

- The student will be able to prepare and maintain examination and treatment areas.

- The student will demonstrate the ability to prepare a patient for and assist with routine and specialty examinations.

- The student will demonstrate knowledge of how to maintain medication and immunization records.

- The student will learn proper identification techniques of how to record vital signs appropriately on a patient's chart.

- The student will be able to demonstrate how to obtain vital signs.

- The student will be able to respond to and initiate verbal and/or written communications.

- The student will be able to respond to issues of confidentiality.

- The student will be able to perform within legal and ethical boundaries.

- The student will be able to demonstrate the use and care of patient equipment.

- The student will demonstrate understanding of the theory of Medical Assistant by scoring a minimum of 70% on the National Certification written exam.

Certified Billing & Coding Specialist

Significant Points:

- This is one of the few health occupations in which there is limited contact with patients.

❏ Job prospects should be very good, particularly in offices of physicians.

Nature of the Work

In the past, a medical assistant working in a physician's office performed both administrative and clinical duties. But as decades passed, he or she performed either one or the other. Now, due to changes in government regulations and standards for the insurance industry, specific medical assisting job tasks have become specialized. In a medical practice, it is commonplace to find administrative duties shared by a number of employees. (Certified Medical Administrative Assistant, bookkeeper, file clerk, Certified Billing & Coding Specialists, etc.)

In clinics and large practices, it is common to find a billing department made up of many people, within the department, such as a Medicare billing specialist, Medicaid billing specialist, coding specialist, insurance counselor, collection manager and medical and financial records manager. *(Fordney, 2004)*

Coding Specialists assign a code to each diagnosis and procedure. They consult classification manuals and also rely on their knowledge of disease processes. Technicians then use computer software to assign the patient to one of several hundred "diagnosis-related groups," or DRGs. The DRG determines the amount for which Medicare or other insurance programs using the DRG system will reimburse the hospital if the patient is covered. Technicians who specialize in coding are called health information coders, medical record coders, coder/abstractors, or coding specialists. In addition to the DRG system, coders use other coding systems, such as those geared towards ambulatory settings or long-term care.

Billing & Coding Specialists' duties vary with the size of the facility. In large to medium-sized facilities, technicians may specialize in one aspect of health information, or supervise health information clerks and Transcriptionists while a medical records and health information administrator manages the department. In small facilities, a credentialed medical records and health information technician sometimes manages the department. *(US Department of Labor, Occupational Outlook Handbook.)*

Working Conditions

Billing & Coding Specialists usually work a 40-hour week. Some overtime may be required. In hospitals—where health information departments often are open 24 hours a day, 7 days a week—specialists may work day, evening, and night shifts.

Billing & Coding Specialists work in pleasant and comfortable offices. This is one of the few health occupations in which there is little or limited contact with patients. Because accuracy is essential in their jobs, technicians must pay close attention to detail. Technicians who work at computer monitors for prolonged periods must guard against eyestrain and muscle pain.

Employment

Billing & Coding Specialists held about 147,000 jobs in 2002. Thirty-seven percent of all jobs were in hospitals. The rest were mostly in offices of physicians, nursing care facilities, outpatient care centers, and home healthcare services. Insurance firms that deal in health matters employ a small number of health information technicians to tabulate and analyze health information. Public health departments also hire technicians to supervise data collection from healthcare institutions and to assist in research.

Job Outlook

Job prospects should be very good. Employment of Billing & Coding Specialists is expected to grow much faster than the average for all occupations through 2020, due to rapid growth in the number of medical tests, treatments, and procedures that will be increasingly scrutinized by third-party payers, regulators, courts, and consumers.

Although employment growth in hospitals will not keep pace with growth in other healthcare industries, many new jobs will nevertheless be created. The fastest employment growth and a majority of the new jobs are expected in offices of physicians, due to increasing demand for detailed records, especially in large group practices. Rapid growth also is expected in nursing care facilities, home healthcare services, and outpatient care centers. Additional job openings will result from the need to replace technicians who retire or leave the occupation permanently.

Upon completion of the course, the student should be able to:

- Discuss an insurance company claim process.

- Discuss the process for obtaining authorization for additional treatment by a healthcare specialist.

- Discuss the authorization process for a patient requesting an initial appointment with a health care specialist.

- Discuss the difference between the terms "primary diagnosis" and "principal diagnosis".

- Identify and properly use special terms, marks, abbreviations, and symbols used in ICD-9-CM coding system.

- Explain the format of the CPT system.

- Discuss the qualifications for a "preventative medicine visit".

- Define the following terms, phrase and abbreviations:

    o Medical necessity

    o Subjective, Objective Assessments

    o Plan

    o Operative report

    o OP notes

- Code diagnoses and procedures from source documents to complete insurance information on the CMS-1500 claim form. (Formerly HCFA-1500)

- State the four processing steps that must occur before a completed form can be mailed to the insurance company.

- Explain function of National Blue Cross and Blue Shield Association.

- List six categories of persons eligible for Medicare coverage.

- List and define seven types of insurance programs that are primary to Medicare.

- State the deadline for filing Medicare claims.

- List Medicaid federal guidelines.

- List services covered under the federal portion of Medicaid assistance.

- Explain how to verify a patient's Medicaid eligibility.

- List Tricare eligibility categories; List six services that are not covered by Tricare.

- Demonstrate understanding of HIPAA Compliance, PHI, and Confidentiality

- List and define the levels of Tricare coverage.

- List the categories of workers covered by the federal compensation program.

- List and describe types of workers compensation available at state level.

- Describe the correct billing procedures for workers compensation cases.

- Describe how to set up a filing system for completed claim forms.

Certified Billing & Coding Specialist

DESCRIPTION:

This course thoroughly prepares students to code patients' medical records correctly and optimize reimbursement for a full range of medical services. Students are introduced to several techniques for finding and applying the correct codes in today's standard coding systems. Topics covered include: current procedural terminology, international classification of diseases, clinical modification, healthcare procedure coding system, resource-based relative value scale, insurance form preparation, Medicare, Medicaid, Tricare, Blue Cross/Blue Shield, Workers' Compensation, No Fault, HMO's, diagnosis-related groups, peer review organizations, and ambulatory patient groups.

METHOD OF INSTRUCTION: This course utilizes a lecture and demonstration methodology.

Introduction to Health Insurance: Introductory course that gives an overview of the insurance industry; what is Health Insurance? Disability and Liability Insurance; Major Developments in Health Insurance; Health Insurance Coverage Statistics; Third Party Reimbursement Methods

Anatomy, Physiology and Terminology (Admin. & CBCS, not for clinical rotations): This course introduces students to medical terminology and includes the basics of anatomy and physiology, medical history, examination procedures, and medical reports. Students will begin developing a medical vocabulary through a study of roots, prefixes, and suffixes, and practices of correct pronunciation and usage of terms related to the following body systems: integumentary, musculoskeletal, circulatory, lymphatic, cardiovascular, respiratory, digestive, urinary, reproductive, endocrine, nervous, and eye, ear and throat. The course also covers terminology related to diseases, diagnostic tests, and treatment of body systems. Students will also learn terminology related to radiology, pathology, autopsies, mental health, and discharge summaries

Medical Laws and Ethics: This course examines the role of the Billing & Coding Specialist and the laws that relate to this role. Special emphasis on OSHA regulations; Employer and Employee Liability; Patients' Bill of Rights; Americans with Disabilities Act; False Claims Act; and Fraud.

Medical Office Skills This course is designed to introduce the student to basic office protocols for the medical environment. Students will learn the general principles to communicate effectively in a medical environment by composing business letters, memos and reports. Students will develop proof reading skills; review grammar, spelling and vocabulary. Students will demonstrate professionalism when speaking to patients. Students will review Medical Etiquette. Students will gain understanding of pre-authorization; and the 'smart card' with a basic introduction to working within the medical team and appropriate roles and responsibilities. Concentration on medical office workflow, medical record management, correspondence, communications, computerized practice management, health and patient financing.

The Insurance Claims Process

This is a course designed to teach the students about the medical insurance claims process. Students will learn: Developments of the Claim; New Patient Interview and Check-in Procedure; Established Patient Return Visit; Post Clinical Check-out Procedure; Insurance Company Processing of a Claim and Maintaining Insurance Claim Files

ICD-9-CM Coding

This course is designed to teach students about the Diagnostic Coding System, (ICD-9-CM); HCFA ICD-9-CM Coding Guidelines; Primary and Principal Diagnosis Coding; Principal versus Secondary Procedures; Coding Qualifying Diagnosis; ICD-9-CM Coding System; Disease Index Organization; Basic Steps for Using the Index; Organization of the Tabular List; Basic Steps for Using the Tabular List; Working with Index to Disease Tables; Coding Special Disorders; and Considerations to Ensure Accurate ICD-9-CM Coding;

CPT Coding

This course is designed to teach students about the importance of Procedural Coding Skills (CPT Coding System); PT Format; CPT Symbols and Conventions; Tabular Conventions; Index Conventions; CPT Index; Basic Steps for Coding Procedures and Services; Surgery Overview; Coding Special Surgery Cases; Medicine Section Overview; Radiology Section Overview; Pathology/Laboratory Section Overview; Assigning Evaluation and Management Codes; and CPT Modifiers.

Medical Documentation

Students will gain a thorough understanding of the medical documentation process. Students will learn the guidelines for documentation; medical records; and laws governing privacy of medical documents. Students should be able to apply ICD-9-CM Coding Guidelines; CPT/HCPCS Billing Considerations; Code Clinical Scenarios; Code Medical Reports; Code Operative Reports.

Filing Commercial Claims

This is a course designed to teach the students about the commercial insurance claim; Insurance Program Comparison Chart; Step-by-Step Insurance for Primary Commercial Claims; Patient and Policy Identification; Diagnostic and Treatment Data; Instructions for Block 24; Provider/Billing Entity Identification; Commercial Secondary Coverage

Blue Cross and Blue Shield Plans

This is a course designed to teach the students about the national Blue Cross Blue Shield program; Participating Providers; Nonparticipating Providers; Traditional Fee-for-Service Coverage; National Accounts; Blue Card Program; BCBS & Managed Care; Medicare Supplemental Plans; Billing Information Summary; Step-by-Step Instructions – Primary BCBS Claims; Two BCBS Full Benefit Policies; BSBC Secondary Claims;

Medicare

This is a course designed to teach the students about Medicare. Concepts covered to included: Eligibility; Medicare Enrollment; Part A/Part B Coverage; Participating Providers; Nonparticipating Provider Restrictions; Private Contracting; Advance Beneficiary Notices; Medicare Fee Schedule; Medicare as a Secondary Payer; Billing Notes; Step-by-Step Claim Form Instructions; Primary Medicare with a Medigap Policy; Medicare-Medical Crossover Claims; When Medicare is the Secondary Payer;

Medicaid

This is a course designed to teach the students about Medicaid. Concepts covered include: Federal Eligibility Requirements; Medicaid Services; Relationship Between Medicaid and Medicare; Medicaid's Future; Medicaid as a Secondary Payer; Participating Providers; Medicaid and Managed Care; Billing Information Notes; Step-by-Step Claim Form Instructions; Secondary Medicaid Claims; Mother/Baby Claims;

TRICARE

This is a course designed to teach the students about the TRICARE Option; TRICARE Programs and Demonstration Projects; TRICARE Service Centers; Beneficiary Counseling and Assistance Coordinator; TRICARE Preauthorization; Covered Services – TRICARE Standard; Program for Persons with Disabilities; Non-Covered Services – TRICARE; Medical Review; CHAMPVA; TRICARE as a Secondary Payer; TRICARE Billing Information; TRICARE Primary Claim Instructions; Primary TRICARE with a Supplemental Policy; TRICARE as Secondary Payer Claim Instructions;

Workers Compensation

This is a course designed to teach the students about the Workers Compensation and other Federal Compensation Programs; State-Sponsored Coverage; Eligibility Classification of On-the-Job Injuries; Special Handling of Workers Compensation and Managed Care; First Report of Injury; Progress Reports; Billing Information Notes; Workers Compensation Claim Instructions; – Patient and Policy Identification; Diagnostic and Treatment Data; Provider/Billing Entity;

Tracing Delinquent Claims & Insurance Problem Solving

Claim Management Techniques; Review and Appeal Process; Problem Claims; Rebilling

Computerized Billing

This course is designed to teach the students the concepts of computerized billing utilizing the *Medisoft, or other* softwares. Students will have a thorough understanding of the software program.

Career Development

This course is designed to assist the student in resume development, soft skills, interviewing strategies and decision-making skills to assist the student in obtaining employment. Optional externships are encouraged to offer the student the opportunity for real-life experience.

Operating Room Surgical Technician

SIGNIFICANT POINTS

Training programs last 4 to 24 months and lead to a certificate, diploma, or associate degree. Job opportunities are expected to be favorable. Hospitals will continue to be the primary employer, although much faster employment growth is expected in offices of physicians and in outpatient care centers, including ambulatory surgical centers.

NATURE OF THE WORK

Surgical technicians, also called scrubs and surgical or operating room technicians, assist in surgical operations under the supervision of surgeons, registered nurses, or other surgical personnel. Surgical technicians are members of operating room teams, which most commonly include surgeons, anesthesiologists, and circulating nurses. Before an operation, surgical technicians help prepare the operating room by setting up surgical instruments and equipment, sterile drapes, and sterile solutions. They assemble both sterile and non-sterile equipment, as well as adjust and check it to ensure it is working properly. Technicians also get patients ready for surgery by washing, shaving, and disinfecting incision sites. They transport patients to the operating room, help position them on the operating table, and cover them with sterile surgical "drapes." Technicians also observe patients' vital signs, check charts, and assist the surgical team with putting on sterile gowns and gloves.

During surgery, technicians pass instruments and other sterile supplies to surgeons and surgeon assistants. They may hold retractors, cut sutures, and help count sponges, needles, supplies, and instruments. Surgical technicians help prepare, care for, and dispose of specimens taken for laboratory analysis and help apply dressings. Some operate sterilizers, lights, or suction machines, and help operate diagnostic equipment.

After an operation, surgical technicians may help transfer patients to the recovery room and clean and restock the operating room.

WORKING CONDITIONS

Surgical technicians work in clean, well-lighted, cool environments. They must stand for long periods and remain alert during operations. At times they may be exposed to communicable diseases and unpleasant sights, odors, and materials.

Most surgical technicians work a regular 40-hour week, although they may be on call or work nights, weekends and holidays on a rotating basis.

EMPLOYMENT

Surgical technicians held about 72,000 jobs in 2002. About three-quarters of jobs for surgical technicians were in hospitals, mainly in operating and delivery rooms. Other jobs were in offices of physicians or dentists who perform outpatient surgery and in outpatient care centers, including ambulatory surgical centers. A few, known as private scrubs, are employed directly by surgeons who have special surgical teams, like those for liver transplants.

TRAINING, OTHER QUALIFICATIONS, AND ADVANCEMENT

Surgical technicians receive their training in formal programs offered by community and junior colleges, vocational schools, universities, hospitals, and the military. The major certifying organization for operating room technicians is The Commission on Accreditation of Allied Health Education Programs (CAAHEP), Other organizations include The National Healthcareer Association, National Board of Surgical Technology and Surgical Assisting, etc. High school graduation is usually required for admission. Programs last 4 to 24 months and lead to a certificate, diploma, or associate degree.

Programs provide classroom education and supervised clinical experience. Students take courses in anatomy, physiology, microbiology, pharmacology, professional ethics, and medical terminology. Other studies cover the care and safety of patients during surgery, sterile techniques, and surgical procedures. Students also learn to sterilize instruments; prevent and control infection; and handle special drugs, solutions, supplies, and equipment.

Surgical technicians need manual dexterity to handle instruments quickly. They also must be conscientious, orderly, and emotionally stable to handle the demands of the operating room environment. Technicians must respond quickly and know procedures well to have instruments ready for surgeons without having to be told. They are expected to keep abreast of new developments in the field. Recommended high school courses include health, biology, chemistry, and mathematics.

Technicians advance by specializing in a particular area of surgery, such as neurosurgery or open heart surgery. They also may work as circulating technicians. A circulating technician is the "unsterile" member of the surgical team who prepares patients; helps with anesthesia; obtains and opens packages for the "sterile" persons to remove the sterile contents during the procedure; interviews the patient before surgery; keeps a written account of the surgical procedure; and answers the surgeon's questions about the patient during the surgery. With additional training, some technicians advance to first assistants, who help with retracting, sponging, suturing, cauterizing bleeders, and closing and treating wounds. Some surgical technicians manage central supply departments in hospitals, or take positions with insurance companies, sterile supply services, and operating equipment firms.

JOB OUTLOOK

Job opportunities are expected to be favorable. Employment of surgical technicians is expected to grow faster than the average for all occupations through the year 2020 as the volume of surgery increases. The number of surgical procedures is expected to rise as the population grows and ages. As members of the baby boom generation approach retirement age, the over-50 population, who generally require more surgical procedures, will account for a larger portion of the general population. Technological advances, such as fiber optics and laser technology, will also permit new surgical procedures to be performed.

Hospitals will continue to be the primary employer of surgical technicians, although much faster employment growth is expected in offices of physicians and in outpatient care centers, including ambulatory surgical centers.

EARNINGS

Median annual earnings of surgical technicians were $31,210 in 2002. The middle 50 percent earned between $26,000 and $36,740. The lowest 10 percent earned less than $21,920, and the highest 10 percent earned more than $43,470. Median annual earnings of surgical technicians in 2002 were $33,790 in offices of physicians and $30,590 in general medical and surgical hospitals.

OPERATING ROOM SURGICAL TECHNICIAN: The educational program(s) subject content must be directly related to:

1. Decontamination of Surgical Instruments

2. Preparation and Packaging of Surgical Instruments

3. Sterilization of Surgical Instruments

4. General Knowledge of Instrumentation

Exam Content:

Roles and Responsibilities (18% of Exam)

Life Sciences (10% of Exam)

Decontamination (22% of Exam)

Preparation and Handling (18% of Exam)

Sterilization (20% of Exam)

Sterile Storage and Distribution (12% of Exam)

Introduction:

This program is designed to prepare the student with the necessary knowledge and skills needed to gain employment as a surgical technician. Students will study all aspects or surgery, including law and ethics surrounding surgery, surgical environment, pharmacology, microbiology, sterilization, aseptic techniques, OSHA, transporting and positioning surgical patient, wound closure, anesthesia, instrument exchange and count, surgical instruments, surgical emergencies, communication skills medical terminology, anatomy and physiology and surgical procedures for the various medical specialties.

Objective:

Upon successful completion of this program, the student is eligible to challenge national certification exams such as The National Healthcareer Association's certification exam as an "Operating Room Surgical Technician, CORST" and will become employable in various surgical environments such as hospitals, surgical units and surgeon's offices.

Orientation to Surgical Technology

This course is designed to introduce the student to the field of surgery and will include history, legal and ethical aspects of surgery and patient care. An overview of the ORST is defined in this class.

Objectives:

1. Understand and discuss the development of the ORST
2. Describe the role of the ORST as a team member
3. Understand the significance of certification
4. Describe and discuss the value of teamwork within the OR arena
5. Discuss and understand "surgical conscience."
6. Understand the importance of laws pertaining to surgery
7. List federal regulations that affect surgical technician
8. Define medical practice acts

9. Understand malpractice insurance

10. Define negligence and defamation

11. Discuss and respond to the four categories of errors in the operating room

12. Define the roles of those who work in surgery

13. Describe the supplies in the OR

14. Describe the equipment found in the OR Suite

Fundamentals of surgical care

This course is designed to emphasize theoretical application in areas of microbiology, disinfection, sterilization, aseptic techniques, universal precautions and the sterile field. A study of standard protocol for the protection of the healthcare worker and patient to ensure that the procedures and treatments prescribed by the physician are safely and properly performed to assist the patient's return to health. Overview of classifications of microorganisms, culture sensitivities, causes and prevention of chain of infection

This course also includes introduction to OSHA standards and regulations

OBJECTIVE:

Upon completion of this course, the student will:

1. Understand basic bacterial structure and physiology

2. Understand and discuss the process of disease transmission

3. Understand and discuss the infection process

4. Identify wound classifications

5. Understand and discuss Universal Precautions.

6. Understand and discuss OSHA regulations as pertaining to ORST.

7. Name the common pyogenic bacteria

8. Understand the significance of Hepatitis B in the healthcare setting.

9. Identify the body fluids through which AIDS may be transmitted

10. Discuss and distinguish between disinfecting and sterilization

11. Recognize the hazards association with the use of chemical disinfectants

12. Understand sanitation and how it is accomplished

13. Understand the process of instrument decontamination

14. Understand the postsurgical duties of the scrub assistant

15. Understand personal protective equipment

16. Describe the different methods of sterilization used in the operating room.

17. Properly load the steam sterilizer

18. Understand and practice safety precautions when using any type of sterilizer

19. Determine appropriate sterilization process for equipment

20. Understand the principles of gas sterilization

21. Prepare equipment for sterilization

22. Describe and understand aseptic technique

23. Explain the rules of asepsis

24. Describe proper surgical attire.

25. Demonstrate proper technique for hand washing

26. Describe techniques used to maintain asepsis in the operating room

Surgical Pharmacology

This course is designed to teach the student weights and measures, basic arithmetic review, accepting and distinguishing medications in surgery. The student will also study the generic, trade names uses and actions of common medications.

Objectives: Upon completion of this course, the student will be able to:

1. Convert to and from the metric to the apothecaries systems.

2. Perform basic math calculations

3. Receive medications from the registered nurse properly.

4. Discuss and understand the basic types of medications commonly used in surgery.

5. List the names of medications commonly used in surgery.

6. Understand generic and trade names of common medications.

Principles of Surgical Technology.

This course is designed to provide the student with skills in basic surgical techniques including transporting, positioning, and draping the surgical patient, skin preparation and wound closure, vital signs, homeostasis and anesthesia.

OBJECTIVE: Upon completion of the course, the student will:

1. Distinguish between general and conductive or local anesthesia

2. Describe the phases of general anesthesia

3. Describe the components of the gas anesthesia machine

4. Define semi-closed or open anesthesia system

5. Define closed anesthesia system

6. Define conscious sedation

7. Become familiar with common anesthesia agents

8. Define and discuss different types of conductive anesthesia

9. Recognize the adverse affects of local anesthesia

10. Recognize classifications of anesthetic adjuncts

11. Transfer the conscious and unconscious patient from bed to stretcher

12. Transport the patient to the operating room or other location within the hospital

13. Describe the safe positioning of the patient

14. Define resident and transient flora

15. Demonstrate proper techniques used in hair removal from the surgical site

16. Demonstrate proper techniques used in patient skin preparation

17. List commonly used antiseptics.

18. Demonstrate knowledge of commonly used drapes

19. Demonstrate proper techniques used in draping

20. Discuss suture material, sizes and packaging

21. Describe the two main categories of suture materials.

22. Discuss and demonstrate the proper handing and preparation of suture materials

23. Describe and recognize different types of surgical needles

24. Recognize parts of surgical needles

25. Demonstrate proper technique for threading and passing suture needles

26. Discuss non-suture products.

27. Recognize and properly load and unload cartridges of surgical stapling instruments

28. Understand wound healing

29. Describe the functions of dressings and wound drains.

30. Understand the process of hemostasis

31. Understand and describe the use and components of electrosurgery

32. Differentiate between monopolar and bipolar electro surgical units

33. Demonstrate the principles and practices of the patient grounding pad, grounding cable and power unit.

34. Describe the different types of sponges used in surgery

35. Demonstrate the proper method for taking sponge count

36. Recognize the consequences of losing a sponge within a surgical wound

37. Understand how a pneumatic tourniquet operates

38. Discuss types of pharmaceutical hemostatic agents

39. Discuss hypothermia

40. Discuss hypotension

41. Describe types of autotransfusion

42. Describe and demonstrate proper techniques for obtaining vital signs and their role in surgery.

Operating Room Skills

This course focuses on preoperative, inter-operative and postoperative techniques such as communicating with the patient, instruments, instrumentation, and instrument count, surgical routines and emergencies and laser technology.

OBJECTIVE: Upon completion of the course, the student will:

1. Identify the components of a surgical instrument

2. Recognize the different types of instruments by category

3. Care for instruments by category

4. Use effective memorization skills in learning the names of surgical instruments

5. Understand the sequence of events in a surgical procedure

6. Demonstrate teamwork and courtesy in professional relationships

7. Respond appropriately to different types of surgical emergencies

8. Understand why a registered nurse must fulfill the role of circulator during surgical procedures

9. Understand what patient care plans are and the nurses role in development

10. Describe the three types of lasers

11. Understand how lasers work

12. Describe all safety precautions taken with laser use

13. Define the role of the scrub assistant when the laser is used

14. Define the role of the circulator when the laser is used.

Communications and Behavioral Sciences

This course is designed to provide the student with skills for effective listening and interpersonal relations, verbal and nonverbal methods of communication and appropriate response to psychosocial stress in the surgical patient.

OBJECTIVE: Upon completion of the course, the student will:

1. Understand what patient care plans are and why they are developed

2. Discuss common psychological concerns of the surgical patient

3. Understand the special needs of the pediatric patient

4. Understand the special needs of the geriatric patient

5. Understand the special needs of the obstetric patient

6. Become aware of cultural and ethnic differences that affect the surgical patient.

7. Understand HIPAA Privacy regulations and how they apply to the ORST

Medical Terminology, Anatomy And Physiology

This course is designed to provide the students with the fundamental facts and principles of the human structure (anatomy) and function (Physiology) through the application of medical terminology.

OBJECTIVE: Upon completion of the course, the student will:

1. Identify the roles of prefixes, suffixes and combining forms in constructing medical terminology

2. Understand and analyze medical terms

3. Recognize, spell, define and pronounce terms related to the skeletal, muscular, cardiovascular, lymphatic, immune, respiratory, digestive, urinary nervous, senses, integumentary, endocrine and reproductive systems

4. Identify boy planes, direction and cavities

5. Identify and describe the major structures and functions of the skeletal system

6. Describe three types of joints

7. Describe the structures and functions of the muscular system

8. Describe the heart in terms of chambers, valves, blood flow, blood supply and heart sounds

9. Differentiate among the three types of blood vessels and describe the major functions of each

10. Identify the major components of blood and the major function of each

11. State the differences between systemic and pulmonary circulation

12. Describe the major functions and structures of the lymphatic system

13. Identify and describe the major structures of the digestive system

14. Identify and describe the major structures and functions of the digestive system

15. Describe the process of digestion, absorption and metabolism

16. Identify and describe the major structures and functions of the urinary system

17. Identify and describe the major structures and functions of the nervous system

18. Identify the three major divisions of the nervous system

19. Identify the major parts of the brain by location and function

20. Describe and identify the structures and functions of the sense organs

21. Identify and describe the structures and functions of the integumentary system

22. Describe at least ten types of lesions

23. Describe the role of the hypothalamus and endocrine glands in maintaining homeostasis.

24. Name and describe the functions of the hormones secreted by the endocrine glands.

25. Identify and describe the structures and functions of the male reproductive system

26. Identify and describe the structures and functions of the female reproductive system.

27. Describe pregnancy, childbirth and postpartum

28. Recognize, spell, define and pronounce basic medical terms

Surgical Procedures

This course is designed as a study of a system approach to surgical procedures and regional anatomy, specialty equipment, type of incisions with emphasis on the role of the scrub technician in areas of general, obstetric and gynecologic, urogential, orthopedic, cardiothoracic, peripheral vascular, neuro, ophthalmic, pediatric, ENT, plastic and reconstructive surgery.

Didactic instruction to include the following surgical specialties:

1. General and gastrointestinal

2. Obstetric and gynecologic

3. Urogenetial

4. Orthopedic

5. Cardiothoracic

6. Peripheral vascular

7. Neurosurgery

8. Ophthalmic

9. Ear, Nose and throat

10. Pediatric

11. Plastic and reconstructive surgeries

Instruction to include the following for each of these specialties:

1. Pathology that prompts surgical intervention

2. Instruments, suturing materials and appropriate supplies for selected procedures

3. Incisions

4. Draping

5. Patient positioning

6. Skin and site preparation

7. Procedure descriptions including possible complications

8. Role and function of the scrub technician

9. Regional anatomy

10. Purpose, direction and final goal of procedures.

Career Development

This course is designed to assist the student in resume development, soft skills, interviewing strategies and decision-making skills to assist the student in obtaining employment. Optional externships are encouraged to offer the student the opportunity for real-life experience.

Externship

The students will gain experience in surgical technology by applying skills and techniques learned in an actual surgical environment with a variety of cases under direct supervision.

OBJECTIVE: Upon completion of this externship, the student will be able to:

1. Develop an understanding of how skills and techniques acquired during the program are applied in an actual surgical environment.

2. Build experience working in their field of study

3. Build experiences with patient relations

4. Build experience with personal and professional relations.

Operating Room Surgical Technician

TASKS/COMPETENCIES

Exploring the World of Surgical Technology

- Explain the purpose and job description of a surgical technologist.

- Describe the roles of the members of the surgical team.

- Identify types of hospitals.

- Explain hospital structure and chain of command in the operating room.

- Explain the purpose of hospital departments on which surgery depends to give continuity of patient care.

- Identify means of on-the-job communication.

- State the purpose of communication among team members and between hospital departments.

- Tour the hospital with attention to areas such as emergency room, radiology, laboratory, blood bank, and pathology.

- Tour the operating room.

- Identify restricted and non-restricted areas of the operating room.

- Differentiate between scrubbed and un-scrubbed members of the surgical team.

Applying Aseptic Technique

- Wash hands using medical asepsis.

- Demonstrate surgical scrub.

- Open surgical supplies (linen wrapped and disposable).

- Don and remove surgical gloves: Open, Closed, Change of contaminated glove.

- Don and remove surgical gown.

- Gown and glove another person.

Performing Sterilization Procedures

- Sterilize instruments and supplies (steam).

- Sterilize instruments and supplies (gas).

- Sterilize instruments and supplies (cold).

- Sterilize instruments and supplies (Steris).

Performing Emergency Procedures

- Demonstrate CPR.

- Maintain emergency equipment.

- Apply fire safety procedures.

- Apply emergency procedures pre- and post-induction: apply cricoid pressure; assemble suction apparatus; set up IV.
- Measure vital signs.

Demonstrating Preoperative Procedures

- Position patient.
- Perform skin preparation procedures: surgical cleansing; shave prep.
- Verify safe environment: check electrical equipment; check sterility indicators; check atmospheric conditions.
- Set up instrumentation.
- Measure and pour solutions.
- Drape Mayo tray and stand.
- Drape patient for surgery: abdominal; extremity; head/face.

Demonstrating Intraoperative Procedures

- Perform surgical counts.
- Prepare and pass instruments.
- Prepare and handle suture material.
- Assemble electrocautery equipment.
- Prepare tissue specimens for lab.
- Assemble drains and equipment.

Demonstrating Postoperative Procedures

- Transfer patients to stretcher.

- Measure suction container contents.

- Prepare supplies and instruments for sterilization.

- Demonstrate terminal disinfection.

- Apply sterile dressings.

- Disassemble electrocautery unit.

- Insert/connect indwelling foley catheter (simulated).

Demonstrating Positive Interpersonal Relationships with Staff Members, Surgeons, Peers, and Patients

- Display therapeutic communication skills with coworkers and with patients (includes handling concerns about surgery and sexuality and about death and dying).

- Check patient identification.

Demonstrating Basic Surgical Techniques

- Apply basic surgical techniques in minor surgery.

- Apply basic surgical techniques in general surgery.

- Apply basic surgical techniques in OB-GYN surgery.

- Apply basic surgical techniques in plastic

surgery.

- Apply basic surgical techniques in ENT surgery.

- Apply basic surgical techniques in ophthalmic surgery.

- Apply basic surgical techniques in orthopedic surgery.

- Apply basic surgical techniques in arthroscopic (diagnostic) surgery.

- Apply basic surgical techniques in GU surgery.

- Apply basic surgical techniques in neurosurgery.

- Apply basic surgical techniques in cardio-thoracic surgery.

Displaying Initiative in Surgical Situations

- Demonstrate ability to scrub alone on minor procedures (OR nurse or technician must be available and in room).

- Display organizational skills (including setting priorities).

- Demonstrate leadership qualities.

Observing Highly Specialized Procedures

- Observe surgical procedures in neurosurgery (e.g., craniotomy).

- Observe surgical procedures in cardiovascular

surgery (e.g., open heart surgery).

Demonstrating Technical Knowledge

- Use medical terminology as appropriate.

- Apply medical ethics and law.

- Describe structure and function of body systems.

- Explain basic concepts of microbiology.

- Describe procedures of anesthesia including drugs.

Applying Safety Procedures

- Provide a safe, clean, comfortable environment for the client.

- Locate fire alarms/exits and explain fire safety procedures in the operating room.

- Demonstrate proper body mechanics.

- Explain bloodborne pathogens and the exposure control plan for staff and students in the operating room.

- Implement universal precautions and infectious disease control measures.

- Explain chemical hazards and procedures to follow in case of chemical spill or contamination.

- Identify other environmental safety hazards, prevention methods, and disaster plans.

Identifying Principles of Asepsis

- Trace the historical background of asepsis.

- Define terms related to asepsis.

- Identify sources of contamination.

- Identify methods of environmental control of contamination.

- Identify the 12 principles of asepsis.

- Define surgical conscience and relate it to the principles of asepsis.

- Demonstrate the procedure for terminal disinfection.

- Demonstrate the procedure for opening sterile items and delivering them to the sterile field.

- Demonstrate the principles of asepsis followed during surgical procedures.

Communicating Effectively

- Identify body language as a form of communication.

- Explain zones of space in communication.

- Describe the types of correspondence used in the application process.

- Explain important factors in completing a job application.

- Identify qualities evaluated during a job interview.

- Demonstrate interview strategies.

- Define terms related to resume writing.

- Identify four types of resumes.

- Identify goals and objectives of a resume.

- Identify the components of a resume.

- Prepare a resume.

- Describe factors important for job retention.

Examining All Aspects of Industry

- Planning

- Management

- Finance

- Technical and Production Skills

- Underlying Principles of Technology

- Labor Issues

- Community Issues

- Health, Safety, and Environmental Issues

References

Bureau of Labor Statistics, U.S. Department of Labor, OCCUPATIONAL OUTLOOK *Handbook*, 2004-05 EDITION, Surgical Technicians, retrieved from **http://www.bls.gov/oco/ocos106.htm**

Fordney, (2004) Insurance Handbook for the Medical Office.

Gerdin, J. (2011). *Health Careers Today*. New York: Mosby.

Learning Express Editors (2010). *Becoming a Healthcare Professional.* New York: Learning Express, LLC.

Lesmeister, M. (2006). *Writing Basics for the Healthcare Professional.* New Jersey: Prentice Hall.

Makely, S., Badasch, S., and Chesebro, D. (2013). *Becoming a Health Care Professional*. New Jersey: Prentice Hall.

National Healthcareer Association Career Descriptions

Swanson, B. M. (2005). *Careers in Health Care*. Canada: McGraw Hill Professional.

US Department of Labor, Occupational Outlook Handbook.

OTHER TITLES FROM THE SAME AUTHOR:

1. Director of Staff Development: The Nurse Educator
2. Crisis Prevention & Intervention in Healthcare: Management of Assaultive Behavior
3. CNA Exam Prep: Nurse Assistant Practice Test Questions. Vol. One
4. CNA Exam Prep: Nurse Assistant Practice Test Questions. Vol Two
5. IV Therapy & Blood Withdrawal Review Questions
6. Medical Assistant Test Preparation
7. EKG Test Prep
8. Phlebotomy Test Prep
9. The Home Health Aide Textbook
10. How to make a million in nursing

Order these books at www.bestamericanhealthed.com/resources.html
Or call 951 637 8332 for bulk purchase

Order these and other books at www.bestamericanhealthed.com/resources.html

Or call 951 637 8332 for bulk purchase

Made in the USA
Charleston, SC
26 July 2013